# How to Have a

# *Wonderful*

# Marriage

## Thirteen Keys to a
## Successful Marriage

# Kenneth and Joy Haney

# Table of Contents

# PREFACE

## by Joy Haney

The following words are written in my journal:

It is Saturday morning, 5:40 a.m., February 15, 1997. I wanted to sleep in today at least until 7:00 a.m., but I just woke up with the words, *How to have a wonderful marriage*, floating around in my head. Prior to waking up, I was dreaming a dream in which I was trying to figure out how I could talk to every girl before she got married and how my husband could talk to every young man before he got married. It was such an intense dream. It seemed that maybe if we could talk to them, we could help them stay married as long as we had been *and* still be in love.

After waking up, I lay there pondering the dream—I remember looking at the clock in the dream and it was twenty minutes to six. Feeling thirsty, I got out of bed and walked towards the bathroom to get a drink. Walking past the bedroom fireplace, I glanced at the clock sitting on the mantle above the fireplace. The time shocked me momentarily. It was the exact time of the clock in the dream. The phrase, "Now is the time," flashed through my mind.

Going back to bed, after getting a drink, my mind was awake, alert and on fire. Ideas came pell-mell. First of all, I saw the cover: *How to Have a Wonderful Marriage* by Kenneth and Joy Haney. Thoughts began to come so fast that I got back out of bed, put my bathrobe and houseshoes on, went to my office, turned the computer on and while it was warming up, began to jot some of the thoughts down.

As I began working, the idea to use an acrostic, "Key to Marriage," entered my mind. Each letter stands for a verb, denoting action, that we used as a chapter title, for only positive action and hard work will make a marriage successful. Together we selected the thirteen "keys" which help make a wonderful marriage.

This book will be an accumulation of old and new material. I taught "Marriage and Family" for ten years at Christian Life College and in Radiant Life classes for many years at Christian Life Center, so some of that material will be incorporated into this book. My husband and I have gathered information and material for many years. As we have lived our life, we have gathered nuggets, sage advice and jewels of thought from others along the way, but have not always kept the source of those ideas. We will do our best to give proper credit to any borrowed material. We wish to give thanks and honor to those who have gone before us, bringing to our attention a wealth of knowledge concerning the oldest institution in the world: marriage. It began in Eden, with the Lord God Himself officiating at the ceremony.

# FOREWORD

*Authors' note:* Out of all the people in the world, children say it best when evaluating a marriage, so we will hear what our five children, whom we love very much, have to say.

"The family that prays together stays together." This is the statement that I have heard my parents quote over and over throughout the years. I truly believe this is the basis for their successful marriage. In a time when there are so many troubled marriages and divorce is as routine as the wedding ceremony, it has been a life-line of stability for me to see my parents truly happy together. As much responsibility as each of them carries in life, they have always made time to go away together, whether it's a drive to the mountains, a trip to San Francisco, or a day at the ocean. Spending valuable time together as a couple, keeping the romance alive and staying good friends has been one of their priorities.

My mother and father's books have been an inspiration and help to people all over the world. I can't think of another subject that could be more needed in this day and age.

*Sherrie*

Although the market is flooded with books that deal with marriage, we need a book that deals with issues that are often ignored. My parents have a marriage that should be well duplicated in many respects. If such were the case, there would be no divorces, there would never be another wife-beating, never again an unfaithful partner, and the list goes on. Instead there would be couples in love, every child would be raised with two parents that were his own, he would know what it was like to hear his dad say "I love you" to his mother, and his mother say "I love you" to his dad.

Although my mother is an author, this is not a subject she wrote about alone, but for 36 years she has lived and practiced it each day.

Mom and Dad, thank you for another great book and for helping this upcoming generation.

*Nathaniel*

We hear people say there is no marriage made in heaven. If they zoomed in on the Haney house, they would eat that phrase. Honestly, I can say my parents have a *wonderful* marriage. Yes, they are so busy speaking, preaching, counseling and working for God, they do not have time to be bored. My father has great vision, and so does my mother, but she is strong by his side believing in him. She is the most positive woman I have ever known. There are a few things that stick out in my mind about my parents:

1. They never give up no matter the circumstance.
2. They go away for a day, just the two of them, for dinner or to stay all night. They enjoy being alone together.
3. They are one in the ministry.
4. Dad believes in Mom and Mom believes in Dad.
5. They are compassionate towards people.
6. They never allow gossip to consume our family.

Lastly, they have taught me that the one you marry is crucial. We are living in a day when so many take marriage lightly, but not my parents. They have truly been an example to me. I hope that my marriage is happy like theirs.

*Stephanie*

Watching through the eyes of a child, I was blessed to see what not every child will see when he is growing up. I felt my mother and father's love and tremendous respect for one another. I don't recall raised voices in our house. I'm sure there had to be disagreements, but if there were they were not in front of us children.

I will always remember, when dinner was ready we would come to the table, but we could not touch the food or begin eating until the lady of the house was sitting down. That rule was established by our wonderful father.

If I had to give one word for my parents' marriage, without a doubt I would shout, "Team!" They were and are a team. They dream together, they give together, they laugh together and they have even cried together. Most importantly, they are still together!

Now looking through the eyes of a married woman and a mother myself, I have a tremendous respect for my parents. Their marriage is based on love, trust, and commitment. With these ingredients you can have a successful marriage. Read the pages of this book and you too will discover how to have a wonderful marriage.

*Elizabeth*

Elizabeth Barrett Browning wrote, "How do I love thee, let me count the ways. I love thee to the depth and breadth and height my soul can reach." My parents are a one-in-a-million couple that has experienced this kind of love. The Bible says we become one with God. My Mom and Dad have become one in spirit. I have always wanted a love story like theirs. The fire and passion of love is still in their eyes for one another even after 36 years of marriage.

My mother is the most virtuous, patient, understanding, godly and faith-building woman I know. My father is a compassionate, merciful man of great wisdom and knowledge. They have succeeded because they both have had visions and dreams which center around God's will. I honor and respect them not only as my parents, but as the greatest spiritual leaders of our time. I have a godly fear and great reverence for my parents. My father is not a man of many words but when he speaks I listen because his words are precious to me.

Their love has stood strong like an oak tree while the winds of adversity have blown around them. Their love is like an ocean, big, full and always giving. Their love is like the stars, ever burning and shining in the night. They have proven that you can have a good marriage even when things are crumbling and falling apart in our world.

*Angela*

# INTRODUCTION

Reading some descriptions written by those of long ago of how marriage should be makes a person nostalgic for the "old" days. Mulling over the deterioration of family values in this generation could make one cynical, but in retrospect, down through the ages there have always been those who violated the marriage vows. Some might think marriage is outdated, but according to God's Word, marriage is here to stay, so why not seek to have a successful marriage even while some marriages may be falling apart? God has not changed. His Word has not changed, so what has changed? Society's values. You can rise above the crumbling values and raise up a "new thing" in your neighborhood. Let this book be a challenge to you to choose the better way. Enjoy the following description written by Bishop Taylor of what marriage should be:

If you are for pleasure, marry; if you prize rosy health, marry. A good wife is heaven's last best gift to a man; his angel of mercy; minister of graces innumerable; his gem of many virtues; his box of jewels; her voice, his sweetest music; her smiles, his brightest day; her kiss, the guardian of innocence; her arms, the pale of his safety; the balm of his health; the balsam of his life; her industry, his surest wealth; her economy, his safest steward; her lips, his faithful counselors; her bosom, the softest pillow of his cares; and her prayers, the ablest advocates of Heaven's blessing on his head. [1]

Life is not always as ideal as we would like it to be. Bishop Taylor causes us to sigh and dream for those perfect moments, but in reality there are some rough storms to sail through, high mountains to cross over and paths of temptation to avoid during the journey of marriage. There are hair-raising experiences, some bumps, jolts and disappointments that are intertwined with the rosy picture that is envisioned when standing at the altar amidst orange blossoms, scented candles and soft music. Helen Steiner Rice captures something of this mixture in the following poem:

"When Two People Marry"

Your hearts are filled with happiness so great and overflow-
    ing,
You cannot comprehend it for it's far beyond all knowing
How any heart could hold such joy or feel the fullness of

The wonder and the glory and the ecstasy of love—
You wish that you could capture it and never let it go
So you might walk forever in its radiant magic glow
But love in all its ecstasy is such a fragile thing,
Like gossamer in cloudless skies or a hummingbird's small
 wing,
But love that lasts FOREVER must be made of something
 strong,
The kind of strength that's gathered when the heart can hear
 no song—
When the "sunshine" of your wedding day runs into "stormy
 weather"
And hand in hand you brave the gale and climb steep hills to-
 gether,
And clinging to each other while the thunder rolls above
You seek divine protection in Faith and Hope and Love...
For "Days of wine and roses" never make love's dream come
 true,
It takes sacrifice and teardrops, and problems shared by two,
To give true love its beauty, its grandeur and its fineness
And to mold an "earthly ecstasy" into Heavenly Divineness. [2]

"With all lowliness and meekness, with long-suffering, forbearing one another in love; endeavoring to *keep* the unity of the Spirit in the bond of peace."

Ephesians 4:2-3

#

IT WAS A day of terrific loss for both the North and the South during the Civil War. The battle throughout the long day ebbed and flowed, at times favorable to the South, at times favorable to the North. At the beginning of the fateful day, General Nathan Bedford Forrest committed the keeping of a strategic hill to one hundred Confederate soldiers under the command of his younger brother, who was an officer in the Southern Army. The General's orders were brief: "Keep this hill against every attack. It must be retained."

Later that afternoon, as the General rode back towards the hill, he saw 95 bodies strewn about on the hill. The General's brother was wounded, and with ebbing strength, he drew himself up erectly, saluted, and said, "General, here's your hill!"

The General represents the Lord; the officers, husband and wife; and the hill, marriage. The challenge is given to the officers of each marriage, "Keep this hill. Don't let the enemy take your marriage away from you, and don't let your marriage deteriorate into stagnation and lose its sizzle."

*Keep* means "to observe anything prescribed or obligatory." It means "to adhere to, practice or perform a duty, to preserve, maintain, guard or defend something." Any corporation, church or home that is successful will be so because it has *kept* certain rules or adhered to specific regulations.

A keeper, (e.g., a gatekeeper, innkeeper, or the keeper of a lighthouse) is the one that has dominion over the area that is entrusted to him. He has control. In this case the keepers of a marriage are the husband and wife. They must hold precious their wedding vows and work diligently to keep their newly formed corporation successful and not let it slide into disarray.

Not only is it important to keep the hill, but it is important to keep the flame of ardent love burning. There is an old book entitled *Keeper of the Flame* written by Ida Alexa Ross who was born in 1885. This title embodies what marriage is all about. It is the responsibility of the husband and the wife to keep the flame of love burning. The following points based on age-old wisdom will help you *keep* that hill called marriage and *keep* the flame burning:

**Keep your eyes on each other and keep your marriage vows.**

Keep adultery, flirtations and illicit relationships out of your marriage. Rev. Billy Graham once wrote,

We of the Western world, on a sex binge never before equaled in modern times, should be wise enough to heed history's lessons. For history conclusively teaches that the decay of a nation inevitably follows the decay of its sex standards. Theologian Paul Tillich, in his book *Morality and Beyond*, stated flatly: "Without the immanence of the moral imperative, both culture and religion disintegrate." And sociologist Pitirim Sorokin has warned that "the group that tolerates sexual anarchy is endangering its very survival." [1]

The book of Proverbs instructs married men how they should meet their sexual needs. It warns against women who tempt men to annul their marriage vows.

The lips of a strange woman drop as an honeycomb, and her mouth is smoother than oil: but her end is bitter as wormwood, sharp as a two-edged sword. Her feet go down to death; her steps take hold on hell. Lest thou shouldest ponder the path of life, her ways are moveable, that thou canst not know them. Hear me now therefore, O ye children, and depart not from the words of my mouth. Remove thy way far from her, and come not nigh the door of her house (Proverbs 5:3-8).

It commands a man to find his sexual satisfaction only with his own wife.

Drink waters out of thine own cistern, and running waters out of thine own well. Let thy fountain be blessed: and rejoice with the wife of thy youth. Let her be as the loving hind and pleasant roe; let her breasts satisfy thee at all times; and be thou ravished always with her love (Proverbs 5:15,18-19).

Remember this: Adultery begins with the first flirtation. Jesus instructed husband and wife to *leave* others and *cleave* to each other. Phone calls carried on with the opposite sex should be businesslike and friendly, nothing more. Cards and gifts to the opposite sex should never suggest anything more than appreciation. Nothing can hurt a marriage more than for one partner in the corporation to become involved with someone other than his* mate, whether socially, mentally or physically. When this happens over a prolonged period of time, the mate who is not involved feels rejected, and the pain of rejection is slow death. It sometimes causes a weaker partner to have an affair.

That is why husband and wife should be careful of accepting gifts, cards, phone calls or anything else from someone other than each other. These are the *small* things that causes a wedge to come between the husband and wife, and often opens a door to

---

* The use of the pronoun "his" in this statement should actually be rendered "his or her," as it refers to both husband and wife. However, in the interest of avoiding the repetition of "his or her," "he or she," "him or her," etc. throughout the book, the authors have chosen to use the single pronoun.

something that eventually destroys the marriage. Jesus said it was the *little* foxes that spoil the vine. It is necessary to keep the little foxes away from your marriage as well as the bigger thieves. Guard against anything that robs your marriage of love, trust and sanctity. Yes, guard your marriage even as Fort Knox is guarded!

**Keep the purity and purpose of marriage alive**.

Over forty years ago, Dr. Julian P. Price, a pediatrician from Florence, South Carolina, made the following statement to the American Medical Association: "The basic unit of a community is the family, and whether the community is strong or weak, energetic or lazy, moral or immoral, will depend to a large degree upon the type of home its families have built." [2]

Jesus Christ was present at a wedding in Cana and it was there He performed His first miracle. God's sanction was on marriage. He officiated at the first wedding, that of Adam and Eve.

And the Lord God caused a deep sleep to fall upon Adam, and he slept: and he took one of his ribs, and closed up the flesh instead thereof; And the rib, which the Lord God had taken from man, made he a woman, and brought her unto the man. And Adam said, This is now bone of my bones, and flesh of my flesh: she shall be called Woman, because she was taken out of Man. Therefore shall a man leave his father and his mother, and shall cleave unto his wife: and they shall be one flesh (Genesis 2:21-24).

God brought man and woman together because He said, "It is not good that the man should be alone; I will make him an help meet for him" (Genesis 2:18).

Husband and wife are to be one in intimacy, goals and concepts. "Can two walk together, except they be agreed?" (Amos 3:3). Jesus said it well in Matthew 19: 5-6: "For this cause shall a man leave father and mother, and shall cleave to his wife: and they twain shall be one flesh? Wherefore they are no more twain, but one flesh. What therefore God hath joined together, let not man put asunder."

The words *ONE FLESH* and *FORSAKE ALL* shout loudly.

A husband and wife should first be friends. It would be almost impossible to have a good marriage without friendship. A good definition of friendship was given by Mencius: "Friendship is one mind in two bodies." [3] This does not mean that there are no disagreements or differences of thought on a particular subject. It infers that the mindset of the two friends will work for the good of each other. The two friends are not divided in purpose or intent, neither do they seek to hurt one another, but are united together, working to strengthen their relationship and each other's success in life.

Remember that true friends help one another. As Calgary Bob stated years ago, "The difference between a friend and an acquaintance is that a friend helps; an acquaintance merely advises." [4] Husbands and wives who care will work together to keep the oneness of their relationship.

There are many things that can undermine this *oneness,* but the three potential hotspots of marriage are as follows:

- Loyalty to one another.
- Financial objectives.
- The sanctity of vows.

Let's examine further these three areas:

1. *Loyalty to one another.*

No one or nothing should be allowed to come between a husband-and-wife relationship. They should be number one to each other. When problems arise, husband and wife must stick together and solve their problems, looking at the problem from the viewpoint of "us" and not "me."

Husband and wife can ask for advice and receive counsel, but the decision must be based on what is best for each other and not just "what Aunt Mary or Uncle Joe thinks," because there are many opinions. Parents must let their children "go" and let them make their own decisions, unless of course, they are asked for help. Then advice should be given that will strengthen the marriage.

2. *Financial objectives:*

Finances is an area that can literally break a family apart. Financial obligations that cannot be kept cause headaches, worry, stress, frustrations, anger and fear. The end result is that husband and wife often vent their frustrations upon each other, making false accusations, each blaming the other, and conversations often erupt into angry outbursts.

Read more about good stewardship in Chapter 8.


3. *Sanctity of vows*:

From the union of man and woman comes the family unit. Families are the foundation of a church or community. It is important to build strong families. Just as a house is not built overnight, neither is a family. It is the day-to-day activities and the decisions that are made which build the structure and determine whether it will be strong or weak.

F.W. Robertson wrote the following:

Marriage is not a union merely between two creatures—it is a union between two spirits; and the intention of that bond is to perfect the nature of both, by supplementing their deficiencies with the force of contrast, giving to each sex those excellencies in which it is naturally deficient; to the one, strength of character and firmness of moral will; to the other, sympathy, meekness, tenderness; and just so solemn and glorious as these ends are for which the union was intended, just so terrible are the consequences if it be perverted and abused; for there is no earthly relationship which has so much power to ennoble and to exalt. There are two rocks, in this world of ours, on which the soul must either anchor or be wrecked— the one is God, and the other is the sex opposite. [5]

Henry Ward Beecher wrote, "Any feeling that takes a man [or woman] away from his [or her] home is a traitor to the household." [6]

**Keep your home holy so that it will be blessed of God.**

The Lord spoke the following words about Abraham, who was called a friend of God and had the Lord's blessings upon his life. "For I know him, that he will command his children and his household after him, and they shall *keep* the way of the Lord" (Genesis 18:19). Keeping the way of the Lord, which is holy, has always been a prerequisite for a blessing.

Once there was a godly older minister who always gave advice to the bride and groom after he performed a marriage ceremony. He would end his words with, "Have you invited the Lord Jesus to be a guest at your wedding and bless your home?" The following poem asks another question each couple should read often:

"If Jesus Came to Your House"

If Jesus came to your house to spend a day or two,

If He came unexpectedly, I wonder what you'd do.

Oh, I know you'd give your nicest room to such an honored guest

And all the food you'd serve to Him would be the very best,

And you would keep assuring Him you're glad to have him there...

But...when you saw Him coming, would you meet Him at the door

With arms outstretched in welcome to our heav'nly visitor?

Or would you maybe change your clothes before you let Him in,

Or hide some magazines and put the Bible where they'd been?

Would you turn off the radio and hope He hadn't heard,

And wish you hadn't uttered that last, loud and hasty word?

Would you hide your worldly music and put some hymnbooks out?

Could you let Jesus walk right in, or would you rush about?

And I wonder...if the Savior spent a day or two with you,

Would you go right on doing the things you always do?

Would you go right on saying the things you always say?

Would life for you continue as it does from day to day?

Would your family conversation keep up its usual pace?

And would you find it hard each meal to say a table grace?

Would you sing the songs you always sing and read the books you read?

And let Him know the things on which your mind and spirit
   feed?
Would you take Jesus with you everywhere you'd planned to
   go,
Or would you, maybe, change your plans for just a day or so?
Would you be glad to have Him meet your very closest
   friends,
Or would you hope they'd stay away until His visit ends?
Would you be glad to have Him stay forever on and on,
Or would you sigh with great relief when He at last was gone?
It might be interesting to know the things that you would do,
If Jesus came in person to spend some time with you.

*Author unknown* [7]

Walter B. Knight tells of how one evening a family sat talking together. They heard a gentle rapping. Thinking that someone was knocking at the door, they opened it. No one was there. They listened more closely and learned that the sound was coming from somewhere in the house. With difficulty they located the noise. A picture of Christ hung in one of the rooms. An electric fan was blowing a stream of air against it. Intermittently the picture struck the wall and produced the gentle rapping.

Dr. Knight comments were as follows:

Think of it! A picture of Christ upset a household! Does not Christ often upset and disturb households where He is supposed to be a welcomed Guest? How many households need to be upset by Christ? Does Christ see things in our homes which dishonor Him? Does He see things which undermine the morals and blunt the sensibility which we formerly had toward evil? Too often, glamorized vice comes into our homes via radio and television. [8]

## Keep the Holy Spirit alive in you.

Jack R. Taylor says it well:

There is no other way to overcome the self-life than through the work of the Holy Spirit constantly applying the meaning of the cross. Without the constant work of the Holy Spirit filling our lives with Himself, we are forever *stirring in the coffin.* Our constant consent to His constant application of the deeper meaning of the cross keeps us in the *position of death* that we might constantly know the *power of His Life.* [9]

Christ has established certain laws for Christians to follow so that they might have a *little bit of heaven down here* in their marriage. Many times His ways and instructions appear to be strange and unattainable. This is because all people are born sinners. Until they receive Christ's Spirit, they walk in the flesh and fulfill the lust of the flesh, which threatens their marriage vows.

James L. Sullivan says,

The Holy Spirit was sent to us because we cannot do God's will with human mind and hands. Man's brain, clever and ingenious as it might be, can never devise ways and means of achieving spiritual ends by especially thought-up, man-made devices. Without this inner force we would soon falter, and even despair. Under the Spirit's leadership we do find ways of accomplishment and methods of achievement. [10]

**Keep positive qualities—work at getting rid of the negative ones.**

| *Positive Qualities* | *Negative Qualities* |
| --- | --- |
| Prayerful | Prayerless |
| Cheerful | Gloomy, morose |
| Friendly, cooperative | Unsociable, disagreeable |
| Kind, courteous, tactful | Rude, harsh, tactless |
| Tolerant, generous | Intolerant, opinionated |
| Teachable, seeking to learn | Stubborn, unteachable |
| Loyal | Unfaithful |
| Have convictions rooted | Uncertain, many ideas —none rooted |
| Self-denying | Selfish, egotistical |
| Meek | Domineering |
| Careful, thoughtful | Careless, thoughtless |
| Courageous, firm | Fearful, weak |

| | |
|---|---|
| Honest, sincere | Deceitful, evasive |
| Patient, calm, steady | Explosive when things go wrong |
| Happy, hopeful | Moody, depressed, hopeless |
| Moderate, balanced | Extreme, immoderate |
| Judicious, fair, discerning | Prejudiced |
| Growing into Christ's image | Having uncertain spiritual growth |
| Generous, open-hearted, forgiving | Resentful, unforgiving, grudges |
| Neat, orderly, systematic | Disorderly, no system |
| Pleasant, pleasing voice | Harsh, coarse voice |
| Genuinely into the Word of God | No concern for the Word |
| A radiant, happy outlook | A worried, morbid look of despair |

**Keep the cards, flowers, and gifts coming year after year and help keep the love, romance and sizzle in the marriage.**

Love is a tender plant that needs to be nourished, watered and cultivated. True love is found in the Lord. Jude 21 says, "Keep yourselves in the love of God." If husband and wife keep themselves in love with Jesus, they will do a better job of keeping in love with each other.

Love is not just words, but it is shown by taking the time to stop and buy a card or something that will give expression to what is felt. Jesus expressed it in John 14:15. He said, "If ye love me, keep my commandments." In other words, show me that you love me by what you do. Showing love and keeping romance in the marriage has much to do with this concept. Husbands and wives have things that are important to each of them. If there is true love, both partners will do their best to honor any *commandments* or those things which each considers important.

From the wife's viewpoint: Once my husband went on a business trip to San Francisco, a 90-minute drive from our house. The music director of Christian Life Center had picked out a piano there and wanted the pastor to look at it, and of course, buy it. He had been gone for most of the day, and when he finally came home, he handed me an armful of roses. I was surprised but elated because I have always loved flowers. The sweet fragrance not only filled the room, but it filled my heart. He did not have to do it. There was no anniversary, no birthday, nothing that would require a bouquet. His gesture made a statement to me, "I love you enough to bring you flowers simply because you were on my mind." The memory is still sweet and brings a smile to my face.

From the husband's viewpoint: I had to travel several years ago to a foreign country and did not feel very well in my physical body. This, of course, affected my emotions. Feeling rather down, I opened my suitcase, and there on top was a nice large card that my wife had slipped in. After reading it, I started smiling and even felt better. Imagine my surprise when, as I started to put on my shoes, there in the toe was another note all folded up, full of love and encouragement. There were other surprises interspersed throughout my suitcase and clothing, which continued to bring smiles to my face all week. In fact, they still bring a smile to my heart when I remember my wife's thoughtfulness.

These are just two incidents among many that we could recount. The key is to be creative. Think of different ways to show love, care and concern for your mate.


**Keep your heart and tongue free of hate, resentment and offense.**

The Lord asks a question in Psalm 34:12: "What man is he that desireth life, and loveth many days, that he may see good?" He then answers it in the next verse: "Keep thy tongue from evil, and thy lips from speaking guile." If a good marriage is to be maintained, both husband and wife will learn to *keep* their tongue from tearing each other down. "He that keepeth his mouth keepeth his life: but he that openeth wide his lips shall have destruction" (Proverbs 13:3). More wars are started in a marriage simply by words that are spoken without thought of repercussion. Some people just open their mouth wide and, as the old saying goes, "let 'er fly."

Learning to keep a bridled tongue requires diligence. Instructions are given in Proverbs 4:21 to *keep* the words of the Lord in the midst of the heart. He further states in Proverbs 4:23 to "keep thy heart with all diligence; for out of it are the issues of life." To be *diligent* means to be "perseveringly attentive, or to show careful, painstaking consideration to detail or important things."

It should be the goal of both husband and wife to keep themselves pure from sexual sins and also sins of the heart, for I Timothy 5:22 says, "...keep thyself pure." James 1:27 states for the man to "...keep himself unspotted from the world." This advice is good also for the woman.

How can one do this?

- Ask for Divine help. Pray daily, "Lord, help me to keep a watch on my heart and tongue. Help me to say only that which is pleasing to you."
- Find a scripture that will remind you of your goal. Then type or write it out on a 3x5 card or 8x11 computer paper. Place it on the dashboard of your car or on the mirror where you comb your hair. Put it right in front of your eyes so you will look at it and meditate on it. It will then start to become part of your thinking process.
- In a nutshell: Prayer, the Word, and meditation help you think right, for "as a man thinketh in his heart so is he." These three things will steer husbands and wives in the right direction and give them the *umph* to triumph through the power of Christ over their weaknesses and faults.

**Keep the fun and laughter in marriage**.

All work, all seriousness and no fun makes for a dried-up relationship. Ecclesiastes 3:3 says there is a time to laugh and a time to dance. Ecclesiastes 9:9 instructs the husband to live *joyfully* with his wife and Proverbs 5:18 says for him to *rejoice* with the wife of his youth. *Rejoicing* is to feel great delight or gladness. It is to laugh and enjoy one another's company, not to endure it.

Some people are so filled with gloom that they cannot seem to get their mind off of today's woes long enough to enjoy a good laugh. Of course, the source of joy is in Jesus. If His Spirit dwells inside, then there will be joy and laughter in the heart.

The story is told about a Hindu who once asked a native Christian of India, "What medicine do you put on your face to make it shine so?"

"I don't put anything on it," said the Christian.

"Yes, you do. All you Christians do. I've seen shining faces wherever I have met Christians!"

Then the Christian said, "I will tell you what 'medicine' makes our faces shine—it is the joy in our hearts because Jesus dwells there."

When husband and wife begin to walk around the house with long faces and no laughter, it is time to call a halt from normal duties. Take time to instill fun and laughter into your marriage and you will both benefit from it. Do whatever you have to do to put that smile back on each other's faces.

Is laughter really that important? Len McMillan, family life director for the Pacific Health Education Center in Bakersfield,

California, wrote an article entitled, "Laughter." In it she states the following:

> Laughter benefits the whole cardiovascular system through dilation of blood vessels and increase of blood flow throughout your body. At the same time you gulp in large amounts of air, which creates a rich, highly oxygenated flow of blood...As the diaphragm convulses, it shakes up your stomach and other vital organs. You get an internal massage or, as one researcher calls it, *internal jogging*.

She also quotes another researcher:

> It is possible that laughter releases chemicals in the brain, beta-endorphins and enkephalins, which are natural painkillers. These painkillers may be as much as 100 times stronger than any morphine or opium-based drug we can take.

Len advocates practicing laughing, even when you do not feel like it. The benefits are myriad and help ease tension and frustration.

"They helped every one his neighbour; and every one said to his brother, Be of good courage."

Isaiah 41:6

# 2

# ENCOURAGE

IN THE BOOK, *How to Win Friends and Influence People,* author Dale Carnegie shares his belief that the need in every human being is to feel important or needed and to be loved or appreciated. He bases his theory on the works of John Dewey, Freud, William James and Abraham Lincoln. John Dewey, who is considered by many to be one of America's most profound philosophers, said that the deepest urge in human nature is "the desire to be important." Freud said it was "the desire to be great." Abraham Lincoln once began a letter saying: "Everybody likes a compliment." William James, a noted philosopher and psychologist in the late 1800's, said, "The deepest principle in human nature is the craving to be appreciated."

Dale Carnegie also shares the story about a man in one of his classes who told of a request made by his wife. She and a group of women were involved in a self-improvement program. She asked her husband to help her by listing six things he believed she could do to help her become a better wife.

He reported to the class, "I was surprised by such a request. Frankly, it would have been easy for me to list six things I would like to change about her—my heavens, she could have listed a thousand things she would like to change about me—but I didn't. I said to her, 'Let me think about it and give you an answer in the morning.'"

The next morning he got up early and called the florist and had them send six red roses to his wife with a note saying, "I can't think of six things I would like to change about you. I love you the way you are." [1]

He said that when he arrived home that evening, his wife greeted him at the door almost in tears. He said he was extremely glad he had not criticized her as she had requested.

The following Sunday at church, he had several women who were members of his wife's self-improvement class come up to him and say, "That was the most considerate thing I have ever heard." He said it was then that he realized the power of appreciation.

**Appreciation is one of the best ways to give encouragement to a husband or wife.**

In marriage you have two people with two basic needs, living together, trying to fulfill those needs. It is important that both partners try to encourage one another by making each feel *needed or important* and *loved or appreciated.* In so doing, both are refreshed and renewed, because the more you give encouragement, the more it comes back to you.

To *encourage* means to "inspire with courage or hope and to animate, hearten, cheer on or up." The "courage" in "encourage" denotes that there is difficulty involved. *Courage* is that quality of mind which enables one to meet danger and difficulties with firmness and valor.

It is the little extra things many times that give that touch of encouragement. It is fixing something special for your mate, like a Starbuck's concoction, and then taking time to sit down together and sort through the cause of the discouragement—then gently bringing to focus all the good things of life and the things which God has already done.

Seek to encourage or uplift your mate by a thoughtful gift, a special note, a phone call at an unexpected moment with a word of hope and cheer, or by going out of your way to do something that means much to him.

Encouragement goes beyond the call of duty. It does more than just build a fire in the fireplace. One writer explained it like this: "It means not only keeping the home fire burning but throwing a pinch of incense on it once in a while." [2]

Remember: *It is the duty of each partner to inspire with courage, to give hope, and to cheer on or up.*

It is a proven fact that abilities and relationships wither under criticism, but they blossom when encouragement is given. You can live in a dry, withered relationship by continually finding fault with one another, or you can grow into a lovely flower, fragrant with possibilities. It all depends on how you treat one another.

There are so many who suffer on earth, so many lives that are torn apart with irreversible pain and tragedy, that it is necessary for Christian homes to become places of healing and bulwarks of strength and assurance. The atmosphere of the home should be conducive to encouragement. Tension, boredom, self-pity and selfishness should not permeate the home, but an air of peace, love and affection needs to be cultivated.

Dr. Leonard Cammer, a psychiatrist who specialized for thirty years in treating depressed persons, said,

> The human being is the only species that can't survive alone. The human being needs another human being—otherwise he's dead! A telephone call to a depressed person can save a life. An occasional word, a ten-minute visit, can be more effective than twenty-four hours of nursing care. You can buy nursing care. You can't buy love. [3]

It is important not only to truly care for each other, but to show that love daily. Husband and wife should warmly welcome each other at the end of every day. If they are apart because of business or travel obligations, the telephone is the next best thing to relay support and encouragement to one another.

Gary Smalley and John Trent say in their book, *The Blessing*, "On the inside we all yearn for intimacy and affection." They also give good advice for married couples. They suggest making a sign which says, "Have You Praised Your Mate Today?" and placing it in a prominent place. They then give a prescription for thirty days of praise (e.g. "Great dinner, Honey," or "You are so kind to other people," or "You make me so proud the way you handle the children") which can do wonders for a relationship.

For one month, praise at least one thing you appreciate about your spouse each day. Spoken words that attach high value to your spouse are so powerful that they can enrich almost any marriage. Be sure to point out things about his or her character (being kind, generous, thoughtful, punctual, organized, and so on), as well as what they accomplish. [4]

The following heart-warming story is proof that praise works:

Larry and Jo Ann were an ordinary couple. They lived in an ordinary house on an ordinary street. Like any other ordinary couple, they struggled to make ends meet and to do the right things for their children.

They were ordinary in yet another way—they had their squabbles. Much of their conversation concerned what was wrong in their marriage and who was to blame. Until one day when a most extraordinary event took place. "You know, Jo Ann, I've got a magic chest-of-drawers. Every time I open them, they're full of socks and underwear," Larry said. "I want to thank you for filling them all these years."

Jo Ann stared at her husband over the top of her glasses. "What do you want, Larry?"

"Nothing. I just want you to know I appreciate those magic drawers."

This wasn't the first time Larry had done something odd, so Jo Ann pushed the incident out of her mind.

A few days later, "Jo Ann, thank you for recording so many correct check numbers in the ledger this month. You put down the right numbers 15 out of 16 times. That's a record."

Disbelieving what she had heard, Jo Ann looked up from her mending. "Larry, you're always complaining about my recording the wrong check numbers. Why stop now?"

"No reason. I just wanted you to know I appreciate the effort you're making."

Jo Ann shook her head and went back to her mending. "What's got into him?" she murmured to herself.

Nevertheless, the next day when Jo Ann wrote a check at the grocery store, she glanced at her checkbook to confirm that she had put down the right check number. "Why do I suddenly care about those dumb check numbers?" she asked herself.

She tried to disregard the incident, but Larry's strange behavior intensified.

"Jo Ann, that was a great dinner," he said one evening. "I appreciate all your effort. Why, in the past 15 years I'll bet you've fixed over 14,000 meals for me and the kids."

Then, "Jo Ann, the house looks spiffy. You've really worked hard to get it looking so good." And even, "Thanks, Jo Ann, for just being you. I really enjoy your company."

Jo Ann was growing worried. "Where's the sarcasm, the criticism?" she wondered.

Her fears that something peculiar was happening to her husband were confirmed by 16-year-old Shelly. "Dad's gone bonkers, Mom. He just told me I looked nice. With these sloppy clothes, he still said it. That's not Dad, Mom. What's wrong with him?"

Whatever was wrong, Larry didn't get over it. Day in and day out he continued focusing on the positive.

Over the weeks, Jo Ann grew more accustomed to her mate's unusual behavior and occasionally even gave him a grudging "Thank you." She prided herself on taking it all in stride, until one day something so peculiar happened, she became completely discombobulated:

"I want you to take a break," Larry said. "I am going to do the dishes. So please take your hands off that frying pan and leave the kitchen."

(Long, long pause.) "Thank you, Larry. Thank you very much!"

Jo Ann's step was now a little lighter, her self-confidence higher and once in a while she hummed. She didn't seem to have as many blue moods anymore. "I rather like Larry's new behavior," she thought.

That would be the end of the story except one day another most extraordinary event took place. This time it was Jo Ann who spoke.

"Larry," she said, "I want to thank you for going to work and providing for us all these years. I don't think I've ever told you how much I appreciate it."

Larry has never revealed the reason for his dramatic change of behavior no matter how hard Jo Ann has pushed for an answer, and so it will likely remain one of life's mysteries. But it's one I'm thankful to live with.

You see, I am Jo Ann. [5]

Billy Sunday, the famous old-time preacher, said many years ago, "Try praising your wife, even if it frightens her at first." It will probably have the same effect on her as Larry had on Jo Ann.

**Another way to encourage each other is to give an added boost at the appropriate time**.

Walter E. Isenhour says it well in the following poem:

"A Little Push and Pull"

A little push when the road is steep
May take one up the hill;
A little prayer when the clouds hang low
May bring the soul a thrill;
A little lift when the load bears down
May help one to succeed;
A little pull when the will slows down
May help one gain his speed.

A little clasp from a hand that's kind
May lift from crushing care;
A little word from a voice that's sweet
May save one from despair;
A little smile when the heart is sad
May bring a sunbeam in;
A loving word when the spirit droops
May help one rise and win.

A little love for a soul that's lost
May help him seek God's grace;
A little tear and a "God bless you"
May brighten someone's face;
A little deed from a Christian's heart
May bless a weary soul;
A little boost when the battle's hard
May take one to his goal. [6]

Do not save your encouraging skills for only those outside your family. Your first responsibility begins at home. Proverbs 25:11 wisely says, "A word fitly spoken is like apples of gold in pictures of silver." In other words—very valuable! Your words can boost and bless or cause your husband's or wife's heart to bleed.

Words spoken will bring joy to the hearer if they are spoken when they are needed. Proverbs 15:23 says, "A man hath joy by the answer of his mouth: and a word spoken in due season, how good is it!" "Due season" means it is spoken when it is needed. Words spoken at a time when your husband or wife is discouraged or going through a crisis will be received like a thirsty ground receives long-awaited rain. The same words spoken later at a party when everything is grand will hardly penetrate the mind, for at that time they are not needed as much. To get the greatest value out of words, speak them at the appropriate time in an appropriate way, and they will be well received. This will boost not only the one receiving them, but it will help strengthen the marriage.

The story has often been told about the couple who were celebrating their golden wedding anniversary. Asked what the secret of their success was, the husband replied with a story.

His wife, Sarah, was the only girl he ever dated. He grew up in an orphanage and worked hard for everything he had. After he and Sarah were married, Sarah's father took the new groom aside and handed him a small gift. He said, "This gift will tell you how to have a happy marriage."

The nervous young man unwrapped the box and within lay a large gold watch. Curiously he picked it up and saw etched across the face of the watch these words: "Say something nice to Sarah." Every time he checked the time, he would be reminded of his vows on his wedding day.

"Submitting yourselves one to another in the fear of God."

Ephesians 5:21

# IELD

THERE IS A poem that tells about a bird that was caught in a storm. It fought hard against the gale, but all in vain. At last it yielded to the wind, and instead of being carried to destruction it was borne to where there were greener meadows and forests.

People, like the bird, often fight against that which will bring them to a better place, simply because of a stubborn will or lack of knowledge. Marriage should not be a hassle or a fight. It is not a power struggle. It is each partner finding his place and doing his duties well. The old proverb says, "By fighting you never get enough, but by yielding you get more than you expected." [1]

A "Yield" road sign means that the approaching motorist must yield to the person who has the right-of-way. This is much like marriage. Husband and wife are both important leaders driving down the highway of life, but if both of them keep going at full speed when approaching a sign that says "Yield," there is going to be a crash. Someone must yield to avoid the accident. The question is, who does the yielding? The one who does not have the right-of-way at that particular intersection. The two drivers must develop an understanding about the highway and about the rule book written by divine inspiration, and develop a relationship that will allow both to continue in the right direction.

Marriage should not be an argumentative relationship, with each driver shaking a fist at the other, but it should be ever improving, developing into a relationship that is caring, kind and strengthening to one another. Both husband and wife are important and necessary to make the relationship work successfully. Benjamin Franklin once said, "A place for everything and everything in its place." We say, "A place for everyone and everyone in their place."

The relationship between the husband and wife is compared to the relationship between Christ and the Church. Ephesians 5:21-33 says,

**Submitting yourselves one to another** in the fear of God. **Wives, submit yourselves** unto your own **husbands**, as unto the Lord. For the **husband is the head of the wife**, even as Christ is the head of the church; and he is the saviour of the body. Therefore **as the church is subject** unto Christ, so **let the wives be to their own husbands** in every thing. **Husbands, love your wives**, even as Christ also loved the church, and **gave himself** for it; That he might sanctify and cleanse it with the washing of water by the word, That he might present it to himself a glorious church, not having spot, or wrinkle, or any such thing; but that it should be holy and without blemish. So ought **men to love their wives** as their own bodies. He that loveth his wife loveth himself. For no man ever yet hated his own flesh; but **nourisheth and cherisheth** it, even as the Lord the church: For we are members of his body, of his flesh, and of his bones. For this cause shall a man leave his father and mother, and shall be joined unto his wife, and they two shall be one flesh. This is a great mystery: but I speak concerning Christ and the church. Nevertheless **let every one of you in particular so love his wife** even as himself; and the **wife see that she reverence her husband**.

You can see that we highlighted portions of the above scripture. Remember that *submission* is "the act of yielding to the power of authority." It means "to be humble, obedient, or to leave and commit to the discretion or judgment of another." Please, examine more closely specific instructions for the husband and wife in the summary below:

The husband is to:
- Love his wife as his own body and self.
- Nourish and cherish his wife.
- Give himself to make a "holy" marriage.
- Be the "head" that will lead and encourage his wife.

- Act as an umbrella for his wife, as Christ does for the Church.

The wife is to:
- Submit to her husband.
- Reverence her husband.

Both husband and wife together are to:
- Submit one to another.
- Be one.

Dwight Small, author of *Design for Christian Marriage*, brings some rather startling insight concerning Ephesians 5. He writes,

> Paul sets forth a mandate in Ephesians 5, which is a singularly complete word to husbands in New Testament instruction.
>
> The husband is to take the initiative in love; he is made responsible for married love. He is the lover. The command is: "Husbands, love your wives." One will seek in vain to find such a command for wives! It never says, "Wives, love your husbands." Some would suppose that this is unnecessary because husbands are such lovable fellows anyway! But hardly!
>
> Rather, the whole mystery of creative and reciprocal love is embodied in this principle. It is the logical counterpart in marriage to the love relation between Christ and the believer.

It is love creating its own response. In loving his wife, the husband causes her to love him in return.

Augustine emphasized the nature of love as chiefly the design of the lover to be one with his beloved. Love creates a void in the heart that can only be filled by the beloved. Thus the lover is ever seeking a closer union of heart and life with his beloved. In the union of the two the meaning of life and love are realized. In Christian marriage the husband is ever to seek a deepening unity with his beloved in thought, expression, and in the shared life. This he finds possible of accomplishment through the Lord Jesus Christ in whom the union is established and sustained. As another has put it so beautifully: "Husbands, thou shalt love the Lord thy God with all thy heart, with all thy soul, and with all thy mind, and thy beloved as His gift." [2]

Society did not appoint leadership to the husband. He was divinely appointed by God. Anything with two heads is considered a freak. Genesis 3:16 says that the husband would rule or be the leader over the wife. "Unto the woman he said, I will greatly multiply thy sorrow and thy conception; in sorrow thou shalt bring forth children; and thy desire shall be to thy husband, and *he shall rule* over thee."

I Corinthians 11:3 also says that the *head of the woman is the man*. I Peter 3:1 states that *a wife must be in subjection* to the husband. Colossians 3:18 says, "*Wives, submit* yourselves unto your own husbands, as it is fit in the Lord."

Christ has positioned the husband to be the head of the family unit. He has positioned the wife to be by the side of the husband so that she can be a help meet to him (Genesis 2:18). They stand side by side facing a difficult world, and when the head or husband would falter or become discouraged, the wife is there to help support and encourage. She does not stand behind him, in front of him or become a doormat under his feet, but she is nestled together with him. His arm is around her, and, with God on their side, the two of them can defeat any foe. Notice Paul used the plural in Romans 8:31. As husband and wife face the world together they shout to their difficulties, "What shall *we* then say to these things? If God be for *us*, who can be against *us*?"

Man's authority is to be used with wisdom and love. Anne Bradstreet wrote, "Authority without wisdom is like a heavy ax without an edge, fitter to bruise than polish." [3] A husband can bruise, maim or slowly kill a wife's spirit by not being a wise leader such as Christ is to the Church. He can destroy his marriage and not even understand that his heavy hand crushed it instead of helping it to bloom into something beautiful. Booker T. Washington said, "You can't hold a man down without staying down with him." [4] The stifling of a woman's talents or potential can put a weight upon the marital relationship, because suppression and oppression always cripple and kill. The husband who places his foot on the neck of his wife keeps them both in a locked, stationery position; neither one can go forward.

It is necessary for the man to be a man and for the woman to be a woman and not become locked into a heated struggle over who is the most important, superior or in control. If a husband does his assignment well, his wife will flourish. She will not feel like she needs to compete against him. If the wife carries out her instructions, her husband will succeed and will not feel the need to continually say, "I'm the head of this house!"

Wallace Denton, author of *What's Happening to Our Families?*, writes, "Men who are men, and know they are men, have no need to remind their families and themselves continually that they are head of the family." [5]

He further states the following in very strong language:

The crux of the whole problem for men is not, "Am I in charge of my family?" but rather, "Am I in charge of myself?" When a man feels in charge or in control of himself, and is sure of this, the question as to who is in charge of the family is resolved. His wife can ask that man to mow the yard and he will see this as no challenge to his authority. He is in charge, in charge of himself. Albert Ellis has well noted that the husband who complains that his wife is making less of a man of him was already demasculinized, and his wife is only aggravating his problem. The solution to his problem is not to get another wife, but to readjust and grow up in his own self-concept. [6]

Your home is a *trust* designed by God to be a testimony to the world to what His power and grace can be in every circumstance of life. The Church is to grow and bloom into something beautiful under the gentle hand of the Lord Jesus. The wife is to do the same under the gentle leadership of her husband, and she is to respond by loving him and meeting his needs.

If a husband and wife love one another as Christ loves the Church, they will have a happy marriage. Marriage should be the greatest thing on earth next to being filled with God's Spirit. God does not squash His Church; neither should the husband squash his wife.

Men are to be *providers* for their families; women are to be *keepers*.

What does it mean for the husband to provide for his family? I Timothy 5:8 says, "But if any provide not for his own, and specially for those of his own house, he hath denied the faith, and is worse than an infidel."

*Provide* means "to look out for in advance, to supply for use what is needed and to take precautionary measures in view of possible need."

Women are also instructed in Titus 2:5 "To be discreet, chaste, keepers at home, good, obedient to their own husbands, that the Word of God be not blasphemed."

A wife being obedient to a husband is not the same thing as a child being obedient to her father. The marriage relationship is not a father-and-child relationship—it is husband and wife. Remember, both husband and wife are leaders, both are important, both have a say in the matter, the outcome will effect both, but the final decision is to be made by the *president* or *head* of the corporation. He is there to help supervise, lead in a confident manner, and make sure that his wife and family are walking in the right direction towards success. After the decision is made, the wife should not harp about it any longer. It is over. What's done is done—whether it was a good decision or a bad one. Forget the things of the past and go forward. A wife should never demean her husband because he made a bad judgment call. He will do better if she will build him up and hold him in high esteem rather than ridicule or belittle him.

Not only is the wife to be obedient, but she is also to be:

*Discreet*:    Manifesting good judgment.
*Chaste*:    Pure in thought and actions.
*Keeper*:    She watches, guards, maintains and manages a good home.
*Good*:    Socially in good report, gracious, fair, honorable, untainted and virtuous.

Notice the ramifications of a husband not providing for his family and a wife not obeying her husband: *the husband is worse than an infidel* and *the wife blasphemes the Word of God.*

An *infidel* is "anyone not holding the faith, who opposes or is unfaithful to Christianity." He is an unbeliever.

*Blaspheme* means "to speak of or address with impious irreverence; to revile or abuse or speak blasphemy." Blasphemy in Jewish law meant cursing or reviling God or the king who was God's representative. It also means to curse God in words, writing or signs. It is an irreverence toward anything regarded as sacred.

God is orderly and is not content with a free-for-all type of management. In the area of marriage, He has set up an order or chain of command that will benefit all. His order does not indicate that anyone is more important than anyone else. It just means that the system which He has established will work well if certain laws are kept. His system also guarantees that the home will become a strong fortress for the betterment of those involved.

Submission is a chain of authority, not a position of inferiority. Which is most important—a key or the lock, a car or the gas? Together they are great, but separately, one without the other, they are useless.

In general, men and women tend to be different in their nature, their way of thinking and, of course, in their body. When you bring these differences together in a positive way, a powerful force is generated. You have the best of both minds working together for one cause.

Submission does not indicate that the wife has no voice. She does, and a strong one at that. She must be listened to by the husband and her viewpoint must be respected in order for there to be a good, solid foundation of trust. She must feel like she is important and that her input is essential.

True submission liberates. Often it has been asked, "When is a train most free?" The answer is, "When it stays on the track." If it gets off the track it becomes bogged down in the fields and rocks. You might say, "Well, I'm not a train." True, but just as trains successfully operate according to certain laws, so do men and women. When you stay on track, you are truly liberated while being protected at the same time.

Another way of saying it is that the wife is to be a responder to her husband's love, protection and leadership. Submission does not mean that personality, ability, talent or individuality are buried, just that they will be channeled to operate to the maximum.

In the book, *Patton's Principles: A Handbook for Managers Who Mean It!*, Porter B. Williamson shares a story that proves that even General George S. Patton understood the importance and respect involved in the chain-of-command system. The author relates that during the war games in 1941, he was assigned a job which involved getting the gas, which was stored in barrels, to where General Patton was located. He did a job that nobody else wanted, and some even transferred to another company so they would not have to face General Patton. When Williamson finally came face to face with General Patton and convinced him that the gas was located not far from his position of battle, Patton ordered Williamson to take him to the gas.

The following paragraph shows his understanding of the chain-of-command system:

On the drive to General Patton's headquarters, he never gave a single instruction to my driver. I did not know which roads to take, but General Patton would not give any orders to my driver. He would say, "Would you ask your driver to turn at the next road." I did not need to repeat the instruction. The driver obeyed. General Patton would not break a command channel. I was in the I Armored Corps which did not take any orders from the 2nd Armored Division. [7]

The blessings are many to those who yield to a higher authority. For the wife they include the following:

- She is protected from the pain and responsibility of a wrong decision.
- She can expect God to keep His promises.
- She is given her husband's name and he pledges to care for her.

"It is good that thou shouldest *take* hold of this; yea, also from this withdraw not thine hand: for he that feareth God shall come forth of them all."

Ecclesiastes 7:18

# TAKE

WHEN BABIES ARE born into the world, they come with nothing except life and a pair of lungs that cry. The longer babies live, the more things they accumulate and take with them wherever they go. When a young man and woman come to the altar of matrimony, they start with much less than what they accumulate through the years. They must make decisions daily and decide what they are going to *take* with them into their marriage.

The word *take* has negative and positive connotations. One reason the word *take* was chosen is that marriage can be a negative or a positive experience. Each couple will decide the ingredients they put into their marriage, whether they be negative or positive. Let us examine the different meanings of the word *take* found in the 1953 edition of *Webster's New Collegiate Diction-*

*ary.* In it we find the word *take* has over twenty different meanings. We will, of course, excerpt the positive definitions, since we have the choice to do so.

1. *To catch through the effect of a sudden force or influence, or to capture the fancy of; to charm or delight.*
   If you are trying to charm someone, you do not try to embarrass him.

2. *To indulge in and enjoy; as, to take one's ease.*
   Marriage can be hell or it can be heaven. It was made so that you could be at ease in it and enjoy the company of one another.

3. *To avail oneself for use or to have recourse to, for safety or refuge.*
   The home should be a haven or a place to run and hide.

4. *To comprehend; understand. Hence; to understand to means, as, to take a remark in the right sense.*
   Be careful how you communicate verbally. Do not say to your mate, "You're inconsiderate and rude," for when people are personally attacked they become defensive. Say instead, "When you do such-and-such a thing or treat me a certain way, it makes me feel unimportant or that you don't care about me. Then I react by saying things that hurt you."

5. *To lay hold; to take root or begin to grow, as a seed or shoot; to unite successfully, as a bud or graft in plant propagation.*
   Notice it means to unite successfully. Marriage is meant to be successful, growing into something beautiful, rewarding and fulfilling.

6. *To adhere or be absorbed; as, ink that takes well on cloth.*
   You were meant to stick together, to be absorbed in making your marriage work.

7. In law: *to receive property as one's own; as, he takes an heir.*
   You take for better for worse, for richer or poorer, till death do you part. Sorry to say there are some people who make it impossible for this to happen. They simply will not work with the system. They continue to abuse, accuse and destroy instead of working together to make a marriage work; therefore, a disintegration of vows occurs.

8. Under synonym: *to accept a challenge.*
   Marriage is a challenge. You can make it work, but you must work at it.

Genesis gives the account of Joseph and his brothers during a time of famine. Joseph had asked the older brothers to bring their younger brother back with them the next time they journeyed into

Egypt to buy corn. When Israel, their father, was informed of this, he realized they had no choice but to do what the Egyptian leader had asked of them. So Israel said,

> *Take* of the best fruits in the land in your vessels, and carry down the man a present, a little balm, and a little honey, spices and myrrh, nuts and almonds: And take double money in your hand...Take also your brother, and arise, go again unto the man (Genesis 43:11-13).

Because Israel wanted to gain favor with the Egyptian leader, he instructed his sons to take the best of what they had and offer it to him as a gift. So should you, as a couple, want to gain favor with each other. Marriage is not the time to hoard or keep the best of you hidden to be brought out only in a time of crisis, but the best should be given to each other every day. Some of the commodities Israel instructed his sons to take with them on their journey are the same ingredients you should take with you on the journey of marriage. He told them to do the following things:

**Take a little balm.**

Balm is an aromatic oil or ointment used for anointing, soothing or healing. There is reference to the balm of Gilead in Jeremiah 8:22. The question is asked, "Is there no balm in Gilead: is there no physician there?" The balm of Gilead came from a small evergreen African and Asiatic tree which was very fragrant and used for healing purposes.

Every marriage needs to stock up on this balm. When the daily wear-and-tear of life erodes your relationship, it is important for one of the partners to recognize the need to get the balm out and let it do its healing work.

To soothe means to lay heated arguments aside, but sometimes this does not always happen. There are times when couples become like little stinging wasps to each other. One says something that stings and then the other one stings back and the room seems to be filled with stings of hate, misunderstanding and gloom. If this happens, someone needs to be big enough to get the balm out and start pouring into the poisoned area.

How can this balm be applied and start working deep within the hurts of each partner? It is very apparent that if the balm is going to be applied that someone has to initiate the pouring. That means that someone must humble himself and be the first to say, "I'm sorry. Please forgive me." It also means that the receiver must accept the balm and not obstinately refuse it.

A sore heals much more quickly when it is small rather than when it is large. If you see small sores starting to appear in your marriage, if there are too many arguments and too many slammed doors, then that is the time to get out the balm. It does not take as much balm for a small sore as it does for a large one. An ounce of prevention is worth a pound of cure. Let each day be a day of inventory. Do a checklist of feelings, emotions, likes and dislikes.

Work together, mold together, grow together, and you can have a good marriage, but for this to take place you must *both* work at it.

Not only is it important to humble yourself and say, "I'm sorry," but it is even more important to let the Healer of hurts dwell always in the home. "He was wounded for our transgressions, he was bruised for our iniquities; the chastisement of our peace was upon him; and with his stripes we are healed" (Isaiah 53:5). The Great Physician knew that mankind would become a prisoner of his own vile emotions; therefore, He came to set the captive free. He should be the most important part of the marriage. It is important to pray every day, "Lord, let us become one in Christ."

**Take a little honey**.

Without sweetness a marriage will die. Sweetness takes on many forms. One of them is an understanding spirit that is able to talk and reason with another. Woodrow Wilson once said,

If you come at me with your fists doubled, I think I can promise you that mine will double as fast as yours; but if you come to me and say, "Let us sit down and take counsel together, and, if we differ from each other, understand why it is that we differ, just what the points at issue are," we will presently find that we are not so far apart after all, that the points on which we differ are few and the points on which we agree are many, and that if we only have the patience and the candor and the desire to get together, we will get together. [1]

Lincoln said the following:

It is an old and true maxim that "a drop of honey catches more flies than a gallon of gall." So with men, if you would win a man to your cause, first convince him that you are his sincere friend. Therein is a drop of honey that catches his heart; which, say what you will, is the great high road to his reason. [2]

Contention is the opposite of sweetness. It is strife and a point maintained in an argument. The person who always has to be right or get in the last word will never have a good marriage. Jesus said, "Agree with thine adversary quickly" (Matthew 5:25). This helps diffuse an explosive situation. Arguing or proving someone wrong always does the opposite of the intended purpose. It makes things worse and the point maintained in the argument becomes more imbedded in the mind, because nobody likes to be proven wrong.

It is best to say, "I may be wrong; sometimes I am. If I'm wrong, I want to make it right. Let us talk this out and look at the facts. Maybe we both have something to learn about the matter."

Never, under any circumstances, gloat if proven right, and never say, "I told you so," with that little superior smile on your face. Remember the two basic needs of each person. You are trying to build a marriage, not gain superiority. Both needs must be nurtured in husband and wife for this to happen. Nobody likes to feel like he is wrong or that he is inferior.

When there is a point of contention, you can do the following things:

*Listen*: Hear each other out without interrupting, resisting, debating or defending. Build bridges instead of barriers. Joseph F. Newton said, "People are lonely because they build walls instead of bridges." [3] Listening accompanied by an understanding, compassionate heart helps to build bridges. It is the hard spirit, accompanied by the stony silence, that builds the walls.

When you listen, try to see the world through your partner's eyes. Walk with him, experience his emotion, and judge the situation by what he senses and feels about it.

*Control your temper*: Remember, the size of a person is measured by what makes him angry. We will discuss this subject more in the next chapter.

*Give time for thought*: It is best not to make quick decisions that affect the rest of your life. Talk the situation out, then wait a few days, making it a matter of prayer, before coming to a final decision. Be honest and open about what is best for the marriage and not just for one of the partners.

Benjamin Franklin said, "If you argue and rankle and contradict, you may achieve a victory sometimes; but it will be an empty victory because you will never get your opponent's good will." [4]

You want to like the person you are married to and that calls for goodwill toward each other. If you constantly bicker and contend, seek to have superiority of thought and continually fight to get your own way, there will never be goodwill between you.

Howard Lachtman, a *Stockton Record* staff writer, wrote an article entitled "Talking Your Way Out of Trouble," which appeared March 11, 1997. Quoting Martha McDonald and John Smart, he included the following tips for responding to conflict:

- Stay calm.
- Don't take an attack personally. Even if it is personal, try to respond from your center rather than react out of anger.
- Be clear. State your case; speak your needs.
- Neither threaten nor bluff. Stick to the immediate facts.
- If a conversation begins, be patient and allow it to evolve.
- Always allow the other side to leave gracefully or make a satisfactory agreement with you.
- Remember that conflict inspires growth and change. It can actually bring about healing.

**Take a little time**.

Charles Buston said it well: "You will never *find* time for anything. If you want time you must make it." [5]

You must take the time to please one another, take the time to be together, take the time to nourish your marriage. Ralph Waldo

Emerson wrote, "Whenever you are sincerely pleased you are nourished." [6]

It is important to schedule time to get away from everything—just the two of you. We have tried to do this once a quarter (four times a year). This is very important if you wish to nourish and please one another, and also stay friends and lovers. You are investing in both the present and future life of your marriage.

Care enough about one other to put each other on both of your calendars—take the time for just the two of you.

**Take a little diplomacy.**

In 1886, Karl Benz drove his first automobile through the streets of Munich, Germany. The car was the forerunner of today's Mercedes Benz. The machine angered the citizens because it was noisy and scared the children and horses. Pressured by the citizens, the local officials immediately established a speed limit for "horseless carriages" of 3½ miles per hour in the city limits and 7 miles per hour outside.

Benz knew he could never develop a market for his car and compete against horses if he had to creep along at those speeds, so he invited the mayor of the town for a ride. The mayor accepted. Benz then arranged for a milkman to park his horse and wagon on a certain street and, as Benz and the mayor drove by, to whip up his old horses and pass them—

and as he did so to give the German equivalent of the Bronx cheer.

The plan worked. The mayor was furious and demanded that Benz overtake the milk wagon. Benz apologized but said that because of the ridiculous speed law he was not permitted to go any faster. Very soon after that the law was changed. Benz proved that the art of diplomacy is getting people to see things *your* way. [7]

Diplomacy is learning to live together harmoniously. It is helping one another, instead of blasting or offending.

"Give me understanding, and I shall keep thy law: yea, I shall *observe* it with my whole heart."

Psalm 119:34

# 5

# OBSERVE

THERE IS A disease called *ganglineuropathy*. It simply means
that the individual who suffers with it is insensitive to pain. A little girl in London held up her broken wrist and said, "Look,
Mommy, my hand is bent the wrong way." There were no tears in
her eyes. She felt no pain whatever. When she was six, her parents noticed that she was walking with a limp. A doctor discov-
ered that the girl had a fractured thigh. Still she felt no pain.

Make sure that your marriage does not suffer from ganglineuropathy. It is important to observe when there is hidden pain or a
break in relations. Pain calls for medicine, some doctoring and a
time of healing. It is not enough to walk side by side; it is important to be observant.

"If I were to prescribe one process in the training of men which is fundamental to success in any direction, it would be thoroughgoing training in the habit of observation. It is a habit which every one of us should be seeking ever more to perfect." [1]

Edward G. Bulwer Lytton said, "Every man who observes vigilantly and resolves steadfastly grows unconsciously into genius." [2] This can happen to your marriage. It can grow into something that will astound those around you.

It is important also for husband and wife to be aware of each other's likes and dislikes. Learn what colors he likes, which foods she enjoys, and what kind of music and books that bring him pleasure.

There is a story in the book of Ruth that tells how Boaz observed Ruth when she worked in the field. He asked his servants who the strange girl was working in his field. They told him she was the girl that came back with Naomi out of the country of Moab. They informed him that she had asked them if she could glean and gather among the sheaves. Boaz then went over to Ruth and began to talk to her. He told her that the other workers would not touch her field and that when she was thirsty, she would not have to draw the water, but would drink of water that was already drawn.

Ruth fell on her face, bowed herself to the ground and said to Boaz, "Why have I found grace in thine eyes, that thou shouldest take knowledge of me" (Ruth 2:10).

Boaz proceeded to tell her that the kindness she had done for her mother-in-law since the death of her husband was known throughout the community. Then they sat down and ate lunch together. When she went back to the field to work, Boaz told the workers to let Ruth glean among their sheaves and to let some of their handfuls fall on purpose for her. Boaz was telling the workers to help her and make her work easier for her.

The romantic part about the story is that Boaz married Ruth. Their relationship started because Boaz had observed or had taken knowledge of Ruth.

Your relationship as a couple began also because you *observed* one another. As this was an important ingredient in the beginning, it is just as important to maintain a good marriage.

Marriage is no place to have your eyes closed, unaware of what is going on in your relationship. The need to *see* is important.

Many years ago an atheistic French scientist was crossing the Sahara Desert with an Arab guide. The Arab believed in God and prayer. When he was uncertain of the way, he would kneel and ask God for guidance. This annoyed the scientist. Contemptuously he asked, "How do you know there is a God?"

Solemnly the Arab asked, "How do I know that a man and not a camel passed by our tent last night in the darkness?"

"Why, by his footprints in the sand," said the atheist.

"I see God's footprints in the things He has created—the sun, moon and stars. They proclaim His power and greatness!" [3]

Marriage has *footprints* or things that are left behind by each mate that need to be observed. The signs are saying something. Not only are the *signs* important but the *substance* of things is just as important. As this generation rushes madly about intent only on what they are doing, often the people—who are more important than any other commodity—are neglected. In the mad dash of life there needs to be an awareness of the needs of people, especially husband and wife.

Miriam Teichner said it well in the following poem:

"God—Let Me Be Aware"

Let me not stumble blindly down life's ways,
Just seeking somehow safely to get through the days,
Hand never groping for another hand,
Not even wondering why it all was planned,
Eyes to the ground, unseeking for the light,
Soul never longing for a wild wing flight,
Please, keep me eager just to do my share,
God—let me be aware.

God—let me be aware.
Stab my soul fiercely with others' pain,
Let me walk seeing horror and stain,
Let my hand, groping, find other hands,
Give me the heart that divines, understands,
Give me the courage, wounded, to fight,

Fill me with knowledge and drench me with light.

Please—keep me eager just to do my share.

God—let me be aware. [4]

## BE AWARE

**You need to be aware of the spiritual relationship of a marriage.**

A spiritual relationship deals with things pertaining to the spirit and has nothing to do with materialism. It involves things pertaining to the higher endowment of the mind and to the moral feelings of the soul. You are joined in the spirit.

I Peter 2:5 talks about a spiritual house. "Ye also, as lively stones, are built up a spiritual house, an holy priesthood, to offer up spiritual sacrifices, acceptable to God by Jesus Christ."

The spiritual house of your marriage must be a sacrifice that is acceptable unto God in order to receive His blessings upon it. It is two hearts knit together as one. In order to have wisdom and blessing, there must be the daily reading of the Bible, for it gives direction. One good Sunday dinner is not enough for all week, neither is one reading good for all week. As the body needs to be fed daily, so does the spirit.

Seeking God and learning of Him through His Word brings honor and approval from Him. I Samuel 2:30 substantiates this:

Wherefore the Lord God of Israel saith, I said indeed that thy house, and the house of thy father, should walk before me for ever: but now the Lord saith, Be it far from me; for them that honour me I will honour, and they that despise me shall be lightly esteemed.

Bible reading cleanses and helps each partner to grow socially, spiritually and intellectually. It is the mind of God. It uplifts!

**You need to be aware of mood swings.**

When one spouse suddenly changes from the normal routine of things, it is a signal that there is either positive progress in a new direction or an outrage against the way things are at present. It is either a cry for help or a signal for some praise.

A marriage that grows and blossoms will do so because someone was aware of the downtimes and will apply some ointment, but aware also of the uptimes and will apply some applause.

Patience is needed, for "this too shall pass." Better days always come.

**You need to be aware that each spouse needs to be appreciated and thanked.**

Walter B. Knight tells the following story which proves that you never get too big or too important that you do not crave thanks.

"What can I do for you, Madam?" Abraham Lincoln asked an elderly lady who had been ushered into his private office.

Placing a covered basket on the table she said, "Mr. President, I have come here today not to ask any favor for myself or for anyone. I heard that you were very fond of cookies, and I came here to bring you this basket of cookies!"

Tears trickled down the gaunt face of the great President. He stood speechless for a moment; then he said, "My good woman, your thoughtful and unselfish deed greatly moves me. Thousands have come into this office since I became President, but you are the first one to come asking no favor for yourself or somebody else." [5]

Remember not to always ask for things, but once in awhile, do something nice that is unexpected.

**You need to be aware that thinking of self only brings misery to both you and your spouse.**

Charles Kingsley wrote, "If you want to be miserable, think much about yourself, about what you want, what you like, what respect people ought to pay you, and what people think of you." [6]

A selfish, whining person is not attractive or pleasant to be around, but someone who considers the needs of everyone involved in a matter, instead of only thinking of self, is much more enjoyable to be around.

John F. Kennedy said, "Ask not what your country can do for you; ask what you can do for your country." This should be the same attitude toward your marriage. "Ask not what your marriage can do for you; ask what can you do for the betterment of your marriage."

**You need to be aware that temper needs to be controlled.**

Henry Drummond once penned the following words: "No form of vice does more to unchristianize society than the evil temper. For embittering life, for breaking up communities, for destroying the most sacred relationships, for devastating homes, this evil stands alone!" [7]

The most powerful men and women in the world are those who have themselves under control. Learn to control your furious passions. Seneca, the wise philosopher of long ago, said it well: "Most powerful is he who has himself in his own power." [8]

Proverbs 16:32 says, "He that is slow to anger is better than the mighty; and he that ruleth his spirit than he that taketh a city." Great men and women learn to control their wrath. If they do not, a marriage will be a continual battlefield. The following scripture proves this: "A wrathful man stirreth up strife; but he that is slow to anger appeaseth strife" (Proverbs 15:18).

Franklin Delano Roosevelt often told the following story: "Two Chinese coolies were arguing heatedly in the midst of the crowd. A stranger expressed surprise that no blows were being struck. His Chinese friend replied, 'The man who strikes first admits that his ideas have given out.'" [9]

Consider the words of Latimer: "He who lacks self-control lacks one of life's best agencies but he who possesses it holds the key to his own happiness and the happiness of others." [10]

**You need to be aware that husband and wife influence each other.**

One of the most beautiful stories ever told was about an alcoholic woman who was gloriously saved. Later, the pastor called on her husband, wanting to win him to Christ also. But the man was very bitter. Contemptuously he said of his wife's conversion, "She'll get over it. She'll go back to drinking again." Six months passed. Then the husband went to see the pastor. He said, "I have read all the leading books on the evidences of Christianity, and I can answer their arguments. But for the past six months I have had an open book before me—my wife, whose life has been utterly changed. I have been wrong. There must be something divine about a religion that can take a slave to drink, like my wife was, and change her into the loving, patient, prayerful singing saint that she now is! I, too, want the thing that has worked the miracle in her life."

Christian marriages are an opportunity to express Christ to one another as the following poem depicts:

"How Christ is Expressed"

Not merely in the words you say,
Not only in your deeds confessed,
But in the most unconscious way
Is Christ Expressed.

For me 'twas not the truth you taught,
To you so clear, to me so dim;
But when you came to me you brought
A sense of Him.

And from your eyes He beckons me,
And from your heart His love is shed,
Till I lose sight of you and see
The Christ instead. [11]

**You need to be aware that anyone can have a Golden Wedding celebration if they try hard enough.**

A grandmother at her Golden Wedding celebration told her guests the secret of her happy marriage. She said, "On my wedding day, I decided to make a list of ten of my husband's faults which, for the sake of our marriage, I would overlook."

As the guests were leaving, a young lady who had been having difficulty in her marriage asked the grandmother what some of the faults were that she had seen fit to overlook. The grandmother said, "To tell you the truth, my dear, I never did get around to listing them. But whenever my husband did something that made me hopping mad, I would say to myself, 'Lucky for him that's one of the ten!'"

"This is a faithful saying, and these things I will that thou affirm constantly, that they which have believed in God might be careful to *maintain* good works. These things are good and profitable unto men."

Titus 3:8

# Maintain

A MARRIAGE IS like two companies merging together into one. Two people with different backgrounds, likes and personalities join forces. The aptitude of each person is often times entirely different than the other. In order for the joining together to be a successful venture, there must be consistent maintenance. Marriage is not just for a short term, but is for the long haul.

A recent national medical fact-finding committee produced a statement on health care that Don Aslett cites in his book, *Make Your House Do the Housework*. In essence it said the following:

We spend most of the medical money, research, and time trying to repair injuries and extend or prolong the life of the afflicted for weeks or months, and almost nothing up front to prevent the problem. A little preventive medicine might add fifteen years to a life, but most of the efforts and publicity are focused on the last breath. Somehow we don't have the wisdom to see the dramatic difference between adding fifteen years to life and improving a few suffering minutes at the end. [1]

Aslett responds to this statement by saying,

Housework is like that, too: Most of the money is spent treating the problem and almost none preventing it. Lots of things demand our money, but housework also asks for our life-blood, our time. You can replace money, but never time. Maintenance-freedom is achieved by applying some smarts at the beginning, when you're planning and building—instead of at the end, when you've been frustrated by it all for years. [2]

Maintenance in a marriage is important. *Maintain* means "to continue, persevere, or carry on in an efficient manner." Before maintenance, the house must first be built. It must be built on God's principles or it will eventually fall apart. "Except the Lord build the house, they labour in vain that build it" (Psalm 127:1). It takes wisdom to build a good marriage, but wisdom is available to anyone who asks, according to James 1:5.

Proverbs 9:1 says, "Wisdom hath builded her house, she hath hewn out her seven pillars." It is possible to build the home and then pull it down by ignorance or lack of self-discipline, as stated in Proverbs 14:1: "Every wise woman buildeth her house; but the foolish plucketh it down with her hands."

There are many things that are essential to building and maintaining a home, but following are seven very important pillars.

## Pillar #1: COMMUNICATION

Communication is the interchange of thoughts and opinions. Hebrews 13:16 admonishes people to communicate. "But to do good and to communicate forget not: for with such sacrifices God is well pleased." This is admonishing the Church to give to one another good things. This is not only good for the Church, but it is necessary for husband and wife to give to one another and care about keeping the lines open.

Although most theologians feel as if Hebrews 13:16 is speaking about sharing blessings with one another, we want to use this in the sense of communicating with words. Words are one of the primary factors of a good relationship. Through talking we communicate our ideas and our needs. Conversation is the intelligent exchange of ideas through the use of speech, but communication can take also take place without speech by means of a gesture or a look. Longfellow said,

He speaketh not and yet there lies,
a conversation in his eyes. [3]

As important as verbal language is, so is body and eye language. Learn to speak *both* effectively with confidence and kindness.

There are many jokes about women talking all the time and men grunting out answers, but there is a story that beats them all. Dr. Joe R. Brown of Rochester, Minnesota, tells of trying to get a physical history of a gentleman. The man's wife answered every question the doctor asked. Finally, Dr. Brown requested that she leave the room, but after she left found that her husband couldn't speak. Calling the wife back, Dr. Brown apologized for not realizing the man had aphasia—loss of speech—and couldn't speak a word. The wife was astonished. She did not know it either.

This story is a little farfetched, but sometimes women can drive their husbands to *aphasia*. Wife, before starting in, remember that the old adage is true, "The way to a husband's heart is through his stomach." Before you want to have a good 'ol talk, make sure he has eaten a good meal and is relaxed. Then obey Proverbs 31:26 and open your mouth with wisdom and let the law of kindness be in your tongue. You will get a much better response from your husband.

The following rules are important in order to communicate sensibly and effectively:

**No double talk**. Matthew 5:37 says, "But let your communication be, Yea, yea; Nay, nay: for whatsoever is more than these cometh of evil." With *grace* say what you mean and mean what you say. Do not make it difficult for your spouse to understand what you are trying to say.

James H. Jauncey, author of *Magic in Marriage*, states the following:

Years of counseling in this area have shown me how imperfect language is to communicate the secrets of the soul. Probably people expect too much of the language. They use it to express the inner desires and yet to hide them at the same time. The real truth is often camouflaged because of pride or anxiety.

The listener, too, doesn't just hear words nor does he interpret them objectively. He colors them with meanings that match his own feelings or wishful thinking. What gets to his heart is often far removed from the truth. [4]

**No putting each other down**. Communication should not be done in a negative or corrupt manner. I Corinthians 15:33 says, "Be not deceived: evil communications corrupt good manners." Paul further admonishes the Church to "Let no corrupt communication proceed out of your mouth, but that which is good to the use of edifying, that it may minister grace unto the hearers" (Ephesians 4:29).

*Evil* is "that which tends to injure, or anything which impairs the happiness or welfare of another." *Corrupt* is "to debase or change from good to bad." *Edify* means "to build or lift up." *Grace* means "favor, kindness or good will."

If you were to replace these four italicized words with their definitions, the scripture verse would read like this: "Let no interchange of thought or ideas, which would debase or bring a person to a lower level, proceed out of your mouth, instead let that which is good and uplifting be spoken, so the husband and wife may experience favor, kindness and good will."

This is quite an order, but the Bible is meant to be obeyed. The Lord did not just throw out words or commandments; they are for the good of those who seek to obey them through the power of Christ.

**No speaking or transmitting harshness**. It is necessary to discuss negative situations from time to time, but it is not always what you say, but how you say it that causes "bombs" to explode. That is why James 1:19 admonishes people to be careful of what they say: "Wherefore, my beloved brethren, let every man be swift to hear, slow to speak, slow to wrath." It is important not to attack each another, but attack any problem with a clear, sound mind.

Communication is transmitting a message. If a wife says to her husband, "Where have you been? I have tried to reach you all day," and does not smile when she says it, but instead reprimands, the chances are that the husband will immediately become defensive and start bristling. The tone of the voice, her facial expression and body movement all communicate a message.

The following statement is true: "An eye can threaten like a loaded and leveled gun, or it can insult like hissing or kicking; or, in its altered mood, by beams of kindness, it can make the heart dance for joy." [5]

**No contradicting one another**. If you disagree, try to do so pleasantly, without arousing bitterness and hostility. Don't say bluntly, "You're wrong!" This normally will bring the conversation to an abrupt halt with someone storming out of the room or engaging in a shouting match trying to prove who is right. It is better to suggest that there may be another way of looking at the matter under discussion.

Dwight Small states, "The heart of marriage is its communication system. It can be said that the success and happiness of any married pair is measurable in terms of the deepening dialogue which characterizes their union." [6]

There will be differences that will arise in the marriage because the husband and wife are both different. They each come from different backgrounds, their genes are different, their appearance is different. They think differently, but author and speaker Tim LaHaye says, "Differences between partners need not be fatal! No disagreement is a threat to a marriage; it's what a couple does about disagreements that determines the success or failure of a marriage. Many a good marriage today once experienced vigorous temperament conflicts." [7]

**Do be open-minded**. James Russell Lowell wrote, "The foolish and the dead alone never change their opinions." [8] The reason for discussion is to sort things out in the mind, look more closely at a situation and to come to a level of understanding about it. The spouse who comes into a discussion with a made-up mind before knowing the facts or how his mate feels is unwise. It is only the wise who can take counsel together and come to a joint decision that is for the good of all involved.

There was once a lapel pin that was worn by several potential voters which bore these words, "My mind's made up. Don't confuse me with the facts." That is the way some participants of certain marriages are: stubborn, unyielding, prejudiced and unwilling to view the facts or to discuss things before making a decision.

Good advice for husband and wife is given in Isaiah 1:18, "Come, let us reason together." The following scriptures show the positive side of counseling together about a matter and also the results of what happens to those without counsel:

- "For they are a nation void of counsel, neither is there any understanding in them" (Deuteronomy 32:28).
- "Where no counsel is, the people fall: but in the multitude of counselors there is safety" (Proverbs 11:14).
- "The way of a fool is right in his own eyes: but he that hearkeneth unto counsel is wise" (Proverbs 12:15).
- "Without counsel purposes are disappointed: but in the multitude of counsellors they are established" (Proverbs 15:22).
- "Every purpose is established by counsel" (Proverbs 20:18).
- "Ointment and perfume rejoice the heart; so doth the sweetness of a man's friend by hearty counsel" (Proverbs 27:9).

It is imperative for husband and wife to hold counsel sessions together to deliberate about matters of importance. They cannot both go about their own business without consulting one another. There must be consultation, deliberation, discussion and joint conferring about anything that either one considers important.

**Do discuss things when you are both relaxed.** The best time to talk things over is when both minds are clear and relaxed, with neither pressured nor angry. According to experts, money fights are the number one cause of all marital breakdowns. Olivia Mellan, author of *Overcoming Overspending,* gives the following steps to help alleviate fighting over money:

1. Discuss how you feel about money when you're both relaxed and there are no major financial decisions to be made in the immediate future.
2. Discuss how your parents' handling of money issues may have affected you while growing up.
3. Keep your feelings about money separate from other issues. Don't make the topic of discussion into a weapon for future fights.
4. Share fears about money, then talk about your hopes and dreams for the future.
5. Explain to each other how your money-handling style makes each of you feel. A bit of criticism is acceptable in this instance. Follow up by focusing on what you each admire about each other's particular style.
6. Negotiate financial decisions only after discussing your concerns.

7. After setting and meeting even the smallest financial goal, congratulate each other on a job well done.
8. Take time to review your earnings and expenses on a regular basis, and talk about your dreams and financial goals. Do this as a couple and as individuals.

## Pillar #2: FAITHFULNESS

Faithfulness is the act of being loyal, committed, conscientious, accurate and reliable. It is absolutely imperative that husbands have eyes only for their wives and wives only for their husbands. Keep the love burning hot and steady. Never let the flame die! Be faithful to one another as long as you both shall live.

Being faithful should not take the charm and zest out of marriage. Bill Ballance says it this way: "An ideal wife is one who remains faithful to you but tries to be just as charming as if she weren't." [9] In other words, faithfulness should not turn marriage into a drudgery, something to be endured.

Being faithful is the thing that God considered to be most important. Matthew 25:21 depicts this: "His Lord said unto him, Well done, thou good and faithful servant: thou hast been faithful over a few things, I will make thee ruler over many things: enter thou into the joy of thy Lord."

Listed below are a few of the many incidents and excerpts from several scriptures which prove that God notices and blesses those who are faithful:

"My servant Moses...who is *faithful* in all mine house" (Numbers 12:7).

"And I will raise me up a *faithful* priest, that shall do according to that which is in my heart and in my mind: and I will build him a sure house; and he shall walk before mine anointed for ever" (I Samuel 2:35).

"O love the Lord, all ye his saints: for the Lord preserveth the *faithful*" (Psalm 31:23).

"Mine eyes shall be upon the *faithful* of the land, that they may dwell with me" (Psalm 101:6).

"Then the presidents and princes sought to find occasion against Daniel concerning the kingdom; but they could find none occasion nor fault; forasmuch as he was *faithful*, neither was there any error or fault found in him" (Daniel 6:4).

"Moreover it is required in stewards, that a man be found *faithful*" (I Corinthians 4:2).

"Even so must their wives be grave, not slanderers, sober, *faithful* in all things" (I Timothy 3:11).

"Be thou *faithful* unto death, and I will give thee a crown of life" (Revelation 2:10).

Let us end with the following scriptures:

He that is *faithful* in that which is least is *faithful* also in much: and he that is unjust in the least is unjust also in much. If therefore ye have not been faithful in the unrighteous mammon, who will commit to your trust the true riches? No servant can serve two masters: for either he will hate the one, and love the other; or else he will hold to the one, and despise the other. Ye cannot serve God and mammon (Luke 16:10-11,13).

Paraphrased in our language it would read as thus: "The husband that is faithful in the little areas of his marriage will be faithful in many areas, but if he is flirtatious and unfaithful in little things, he is unfaithful in all. The same goes for the wife. If the husband or wife cannot be faithful to their partner in marriage, then how can they experience the true riches of God? No husband can serve two women, neither can a wife serve two men. They will either hate the one and love the other."

Dr. Chuck Swindoll shares in his book, *Strike the Original Match*, the following principles that enhance commitment or faithfulness to one another:

1. *No Conflict is Unsolvable*. Christian marriages have conflicts, but they are not beyond solution. Faithfulness or commitment to one another does not erase our humanity. There will be times of tension, tears, struggle, disagreement and impatience, but they are solvable. Do not walk out the door when they come; work at solving them.

2. *Persistence Pays Off.* Working through is harder than walking out, but this is God's way. Why does persistence pay off?

   a. It is the continual counsel of scripture.

   b. One's own growth in Christ is strengthened.

   c. Working through things that needed to be changed. To walk out means that we take our same hang-ups into the next relationship.

   d. The testimony of Christ before the public is enhanced.

   e. Children in the family remain more secure, stable, and balanced.

   f. Rabbi Grollman says that divorce can be more traumatic than death. The big difference is, death has closure, it's over; with divorce it is never over.

3. *God Defends Unselfish Commitment.* Being committed to one's mate is not a matter of demanding rights, but on the contrary, it is the releasing of one's rights.

   a. I Corinthians 7:3-4 says, "Let the husband render unto the wife due benevolence: and likewise also the wife unto the husband. The wife hath not power of her own body, but the husband: and likewise also the husband hath not power of his own body, but the wife."

   b. God's way is to surrender your rights.

   c. Remember: Marriage is a *duet* not a *solo.*

There is a pathetic story told about the Danks family: the family who gave to the world the old song, "Silver Threads

Among the Gold." In 1874, Mr. and Mrs. Danks, with their little brood of children, were a very dedicated and devoted couple. Both were in their early thirties. Mr. Danks was a songwriter of growing reputation. The couple had beautiful dreams of going down life's pathway and growing old together. In the atmosphere of this joyous anticipation the song was born and became universally popular.

But marital discord came into the Danks' household. Separation followed. Mr. Danks died in 1903. He was found dead, kneeling beside his bed. On an old copy of the famous song he had written these words: "It's hard to grow old alone!"

## Pillar #3: INTEGRITY

Without integrity a marriage will always be shaky. It is impossible to build a foundation of any worth without it. Integrity is the act of being honest, undivided and complete. It is the command of God to live honestly in all things. The request of each married couple should be: "Pray for us: for we trust we have a good conscience, in all things willing to live honestly" (Hebrews 13:18).

If you are not willing to live honestly with truth and integrity, then you should not get married. Marriages built on lies and deceit will end in disaster or coast along with much heartache. You cannot have a happy life where there is deceit, for as someone said years ago, "A shady business never produces a sunny life."

The Bible commands that people "Lie not one to another" (Colossians 3:9). Lying should be avoided, but if it is a problem, there needs to be honest discussion and help sought in this area. If you cannot trust one another, you have nothing to build upon, and eventually all lies will be revealed anyway. The old adage is true, "Lies, like chickens, have a way of coming home to roost." You cannot hide from a lie.

It is also miserable living a lie. Margaret Fielty, a director of adult education in Fitchburg, Massachusetts, in recalling various cases with which she dealt over the years, tells of a man who came to her, admitting that even his wife did not know he could not read. For eleven years he had been holding a newspaper for an hour every night, pretending to read it. Finally, he just could not stand the misery any longer.

That is the way many couples are. They hide things from each other because they are afraid of being laughed at, scorned or misunderstood. There is pride, feelings and ego involved. Isn't that why most people lie—to save face or to make something appear to be that which is not? Other people lie to cover up wrong doings, but then again, why do they do it? They want to appear a certain way in the eyes of someone else or hide a wrongdoing without paying the consequence. They are afraid of the ramifications, therefore, a lie is told.

It is so strange when two people who are intimate with one another, who choose to live together with each other for the rest of their lives, and are close together in so many ways, are yet so far apart—afraid to bare their heart or afraid to be honest. So they, like the man who held the newspaper up for one hour every night for eleven years to impress his wife, keep hiding from truth and end up leading a miserable existence.

Work at making it easy to be open with one another. Tear down walls and build bridges of understanding and love. Encourage one another to open up and talk, so that lies will be far from the marriage.

## Pillar #4: CHEERFULNESS

Notice that Jesus came to bring cheer. He said, "Be of good cheer," to several people with whom He had contact. Note the following scriptures:

- Matthew 9:2: "Jesus seeing their faith said unto the sick of the palsy; Son, *be of good cheer;* thy sins be forgiven thee."
- Matthew 14:27: "But straightway Jesus spake unto them [the disciples], saying, *Be of good cheer;* it is I; be not afraid."
- John 16:33: "These things I have spoken unto you, that in me ye might have peace. In the world ye shall have tribulation; but *be of good cheer;* I have overcome the world."
- Acts 23:11: "And the night following the Lord stood by him, and said, *Be of good cheer,* Paul: for as thou hast testified of me in Jerusalem, so must thou bear witness also at Rome."

Jesus wants husbands and wives to "Be of good cheer!"

Continual bad moods in a marriage will breed discontentment and disrespect. They are to be avoided like the plague. If a husband and wife want their marriage to thrive, they will both work at being cheerful. Richter, the wise philosopher, said, "Cheerfulness or joyfulness is the atmosphere under which all things thrive." [10]

Maltbie D. Babcock wrote,

Have you ever had your day suddenly turned sunshiny because of a cheerful word? Have you ever wondered if this could be the same world, because some one had been unexpectedly kind to you? You can make today the same for everybody. It is only a question of a little imagination, a little time and trouble. Think now "what can I do today to make somebody [husband or wife] happy?" [11]

The people who are cheerful seem to be the ones who get more done, have more people respond to them and have the most influence. One unknown writer said it like this, to which we agree, "Power dwells with cheerfulness." [12]

When the day is gloomy, learn to sing some happy song. A good story, a hearty laugh and the sweet pleasantries of life act as lubricants which oil life's machinery so that life is a lot more worth living. Someone might say, "Well, I'm just naturally a grouch." That may be true, but anyone can change. Samuel Smiles wrote, "The habit of viewing things cheerfully, and thinking about life hopefully, may be made to grow up in us like any other habit." [13]

A happy disposition is worth more to its possessor than all the gold mines in the world. If you haven't come into the world with one, try to acquire it. Whatever happens, just make up your mind that you are going to be cheerful; that you will not add to the gloom and unhappiness already in the world by going about with a long, gloomy face, but will scatter laughter and sunshine wherever you go. When things go wrong, keep sweet. When they go right, keep sweet. When people denounce and abuse you, keep sweet, keep pleasant. No matter what happens. In this way you will do more good than any multimillionaire could do with all his money. You will be happy yourself, and you will make others happy. You will treble your chances of success and popularity, for every one loves and admires the cheerful, sunny soul. All doors fly open to him, because wherever he goes, "he sweetens sour customers." [14]

Henry Van Dyke wrote, "There is no personal charm so great as the charm of a cheerful and happy temperament." [15]

Several years ago something happened to a movie millionaire, Nicholas Schenck. He was boarding the yacht of Tom Meighan when he noticed a slip of a girl standing near the edge of the dock. The story goes like this: "For some inexplicable reason," Schenck later recalled, "I had an uncontrollable impulse to push her into the water. To my horror—I did. I had no idea if she could swim. I expected an infuriated young woman. Instead, she came to the surface, blinked the water out of her eyes and smiled a brilliant smile.

"I said to myself, 'That's the girl I'm going to marry!'" and he did. [16]

You never know when your cheerfulness will make you richer than you already are!

## Pillar #5: LOVE AND HONOR

Romans 12:10 is good advice for the husband and wife. "Be kindly affectioned one to another with brotherly love; in honour preferring one another." Affection and love are not luxuries in a marriage—they are necessities; without them the marriage will be only an empty shell of deadness.

Dr. Rene Spitz of New York compared two sets of infants in two institutions. In one institution called "Nursery," the mothers took care of their own infants. In the second called "Foundinghome," one overworked nurse took care of twelve infants. The test results: "Nursery" babies began with an IQ of 101.5. This rose in one year to 105. "Founding" babies started with a 124 IQ, but declined to 45 within two years. Also in two years, 37% of "Founding" children died; but in five years, "Nursery" did not lose a child.

Love and affection made the difference. Everything blooms where there is love. There was once a woman who was married to a man who was very austere and lacking in affection. He wrote out a list of rules for her to do. He forced her to get up every morning at five o'clock, cook his breakfast, and serve it at six o'clock sharp. He made her wait on him and was exacting in his demands on her time. Her life was made miserable trying to satisfy the demands of her husband. Finally he died.

After a few years she married again. This time she married a man whom she loved very much. One day while clearing out some old papers, she came across the strict set of rules her former husband had written out for her to obey. Carefully she read them over. "Get up at five. Serve breakfast at six sharp." On and on she read.

Then she stopped and thought, and realized that she was fulfilling every single one of her deceased husband's demands for her new husband, but she had not realized it because this time she was doing it for love's sake. It was not demanded of her in a cold way, so it was not difficult to perform her duties. Love and honor took the rough edges off of routine duty.

## Pillar #6: KINDNESS

Kindness is love active.

Oh, the comfort, the inexpressible comfort of feeling safe with a person, having neither to weigh thoughts nor measure words, but pour them all right out just as they are, chaff and grain together, knowing that a faithful hand will take and sift them, keep what is worth keeping, and then with the breath of kindness blow the rest away. [17]

Kindness is blowing away the things that some people grab and use eagerly to try to build a monument of hate, misunderstanding and resentment. Whenever a husband and wife are truly sincere and are trying to work out a problem, it is necessary for each one to be able to speak from the heart, with everything all mixed up together. The kind heart will keep what is worth keeping and throw the rest away.

Ephesians 4:32 says, "Be ye *kind* one to another."

Francis E. Willard believed that kindness was a habit and wrote the following:

Just as you now play a piece without the music and do not think what notes you strike, though once you picked them out by slow and patient toil, so if you begin of set purpose, you will learn the law of kindness in utterance so perfectly that it will be second nature to you, and make more music in your life than all the songs the sweetest voice has ever sung. [18]

You never know what the day will hold. Better to bite the tongue in the morning than to feel the prick of bad conscience all day because of some angry, unkind words that were spoken in an unguarded moment.

Margaret Sangster wrote the following thought-provoking poem:

"In The Morning"

If I had known in the morning
How wearily all the day
The words unkind
Would trouble my mind,
I said when you went away,
I had been more careful, darling,
Nor given you needless pain,
But we vex our own
With look and tone
We might never take back again.

For though in the quiet evening
You might give me the kiss of peace,
Yet it might be
That never for me
The pain of the heart should cease.
How many go forth in the morning
That never come back at night!
And hearts have been broken
For harsh words spoken

That sorrow can ne'er set right.

We have careful thoughts for the stranger,
And smiles for the sometimes guest,
But oft for "our own"
The bitter tone,
Though we love "our own" the best.
Ah, lips with the curve impatient!
Ah, brow with that look of scorn!
'Twere a cruel fate
Were the night too late
To undo the work of morn. [19]

You can study more about kindness in a book Joy Haney has written, *The Magical Gift of Kindness*.

## Pillar #7: STEWARDSHIP

Good stewardship is taking charge or controlling well all that which is placed in a person's hand or life. To do nothing is the worst kind of stewardship. Jesus gave a stern rebuke to the man who did nothing with what he was given. The story He told in Matthew 25 was about the man who traveled into a far country and left his servants in charge of his goods. He gave to one man five talents, another he gave two and the third man he gave one. The men with five and two talents worked with what they had and increased what they had been given. When the traveling man asked the third man what he had done with his one talent, he answered, "Lord, I knew thee that thou art an hard man, reaping where thou hast not sown, and gathering where thou hast not strawed: And I was afraid, and went and hid thy talent in the earth: lo, there thou hast that is thine" (Matthew 25:24-25).

This angered the lord and he said to him,

Thou wicked and slothful servant, thou knewest that I reap where I sowed not, and gather where I have not strawed: Thou oughtest therefore to have put my money to the exchangers, and then at my coming I should have received mine own with usury. Take therefore the talent from him, and give it unto him which hath ten talents...And cast ye the unprofitable servant into outer darkness: there shall be weeping and gnashing of teeth (Matthew 25:26-28,30).

It is important that both husband and wife consider their marriage to be an investment and that both of their efforts are important. Edward Everett Hale wrote the following which applies to the importance of involvement by both partners:

I am only one,
But still I am one.
I cannot do everything,
But still I can do something;
And because I can not do everything,

I will not refuse to do the something that I can do. [20]

Each partner adds something uniquely different to the investment called marriage. The gifts of both husband and wife are required to make it successful. Matthew Henry wrote, "We must make the most of our gifts. The steward's duty is to serve well. Idleness is a sin. Life is a journey, and should be upward, which means struggle." [21]

Some people want a good marriage without putting anything into it. They are like the father who attended church with his little boy. There was nothing in the service which the faultfinding father liked. As he walked home with his boy, he criticized the minister and his sermon. He found fault with the choir and with everything in general. The boy had noticed that when the offering was taken, his father had put a dime into the collection plate. So he asked his father, "Well, Dad, what can you expect for a dime?"

Not giving your best, getting by with less in the area of attitudes and feelings, is the death of love. There is work involved and yes, at times struggle, to get to where you want to go, but how bad do you want a good marriage? You will get what you put into it.

One of the most important areas of stewardship is to *guard* the investment you have made in your marriage relationship. Edgar Guest says it well in the following poem:

"To the June Bride"

The groom is at the altar, and the organ's playing low,
Young and old, your friends are waiting, they are sitting row
by row.
Now your girlhood's all behind you, in a few brief minutes
more
You'll be wife to him who's waiting, through the years that
lie before.

Oh, I say it not to daunt you, but to strengthen you for fate,
In the distance for your coming many heavy trials wait.
Whoso enters into marriage takes a very solemn vow
To be faithful to the other when the days are not as now.

Arm in arm you'll walk together through the lane of many
years.
Side by side you'll reap life's pleasures, side by side you'll
shed your tears;
'Tis a long road you'll be faring, for I've journeyed half the
way,
But if love and faith sustain you, you will triumph, come what
may.

There's the happy time of marriage, but to every man and
wife
Also come the hurts and sorrows and the bitterness of life;
For by these your faith is tested, 'tis by these your love shall
grow,

And my prayer is love shall guide you wheresoever you shall go. [22]

Be a good steward and guard your marriage vows well, and the quality of your life will deepen. You will attain to heights never before envisioned. These words, penned over 75 years ago, are still true today: "Stewardship makes every job a divine mission. Stewardship is not optional for the Christian; it is essential. Stewardship is not primarily to heighten the giving but to deepen the living." [23]

"Happy is he that condemneth not himself in that thing which he alloweth."

Romans 14:23

#

# 7

MARRIAGE SHOULD NOT be a prison, but a palace. It should be a haven instead of a hell, a delight instead of a disaster; it should be a place of triumph and not a place of terror. Marriage is a union between two people who are committed to love, honor and cherish one another. It should not be a place to choke, smother and hurt one another. The commitment of love should be strong enough to allow each person to soar and become. Husbands and wives should be allowed freedom to become the people they were created to be; marriage should not make them feel trapped or unfulfilled.

*Allow* means "to approve or sanction something." Consider the following areas that could enrich the *climate* of the marriage by allowing each other to fly:

**Allow Expression**.

This, of course, is only to be done if it does not hurt one another or demoralize or undermine the marriage. Restrain from squashing one another, but allow each other to bloom or to become the person God intended.

There is more strength and support when both husband and wife are involved than if each stands alone. The Scripture speaks of one putting a thousand to flight but two putting ten thousand to flight. Use that strength for positive expression that will benefit the world. Marriage should be the launching pad for greater things. The union of two souls working and cheering one another on will reap great benefits. The original plan for the knitting together of two hearts was so that each could fly! Henry Ward Beecher once said, "Well-married, a man [woman] is winged: ill-matched, he [she] is shackled." [1] So true!

**Allow Growth**.

Growth is a process. It is needful for husband and wife to learn to be patient while there is growth in progress. Growing times are sometimes painful times. Just as a tiny seed must penetrate or push that heavy clod of dirt off its back, so does the person who is growing. There is effort and discipline involved. This is where husband and wife both have an obligation to one another to be careful not to smash that small sprout of growth. A spoken word of discouragement or ridicule can cause the new growth to wither.

Patience is involved. For things to grow, there must be a waiting period. Ralph Waldo Emerson wrote, "Adopt the pace of nature: her secret is patience." [2] Sometimes a young couple will see an older couple who has a good marriage, and the younger people want the same thing *now*. It takes time to build a good, solid marriage. Benjamin Franklin said, "He that can have patience can have what he will." [3]

While you are waiting for the seed of your love to grow into something beautiful and mature, do not just wait, but hustle. Thomas A. Edison wrote, "Everything comes to him who hustles while he waits." [4] Good marriages do not evolve by couples just twiddling their thumbs, hoping that everything will turn out all right. They, like the farmer, determine what needs to be grown in their field. Then they need to till the ground, plant the seed, water it, work at keeping the weeds out and watch it grow. You can have the best crop of love available if you work at it.

**Allow Dreams**.

A good marriage will awaken the best in each other. Ralph Waldo Emerson said it so well: "The profoundest thought or passion sleeps as in a mine, until an equal mind and heart finds and publishes it." [5] Look for the "hidden" jewel that is in your mate and help to bring it forth, for when you help someone else (in this case, your mate) you help yourself most. When you help another person flourish and blossom, the fragrance of their success perfumes all that you do.

Sometimes life becomes just a series of keeping appointments, going to the job, and taking care of all the necessary things which make the world go round, such that dreams are put on the back burner. Husbands and wives get on a merry-go-round and see each other spinning by and inside they are lonely and unfulfilled, just doing all that life requires them to do. But there is something more to living!

There are dreams, passions and ideals that need to be considered and entwined into the fabric of life. Automobiles are cold steel, houses are brick and wood, clothes are cotton and wool; all of these things are "dead" objects which have no feelings or pulsating passion. But much of life is given to attaining them, while dreams that help "live" objects, such as people, remain untouched because of the emphasis put on the attainment of things.

Encourage one another to let the inner *symphony of dreams* come forth to bless a world and bring honor and glory to Jesus Christ. Take the time and allow this to happen.

**Allow Forgiveness.**

*The Watchman Examiner* contained the following words, which should be memorized or thought upon often by every couple:

He who holds a grudge injures himself more than the one against whom he cherishes the spirit of spite. Hatred and malice, like anger and worry, are injurious to the body, since they poison the blood. More serious is the injury which they bring to personality. A bad spirit paralyzes the powers which should help to refine our natures and make for finer character. And this spirit of ill will has a strange way of increasing, for "a grudge is the only thing that does not get better when it is nursed." [6]

Sometimes it is hard to forgive because of the hurts involved, but if husband and wife could reach into the Word and see how the Lord Jesus forgave, then they could forgive more easily. Society is not the plumbline for marriages, the Word of God is. Jesus cried on the cross, "Father, forgive them for they know not what they do." He did this for those who did not deserve forgiving.

Walter B. Knight tells the story about a man who was deeply convicted of sin and realized his need of the Saviour. Restlessly he wandered one night along a country road, seeking relief for his misery. Wearily he sat down beside a hedge. After sitting there for a while, he heard two girls talking on the other side of the hedge. They were discussing a sermon they had heard. "I will never forget the thing the minister said in the sermon. It gave me hope and encouragement," one girl said.

"What was it?" eagerly asked the other girl.

"The world always says that you make your own bed, and you must lie in it, but One greater than the world has said, 'Take up thy bed, and walk. Thy sins be forgiven!'" When the distressed man heard those wondrous words, he called upon Jesus and felt his burden taken away.

Every marriage will have its times of hurts and misunderstandings, some more deeply than others. The choice lies in the hearts of the two involved. There must be forgiveness on the part of each mate for there to be true relief and happiness or for broken trusts and hearts to be mended.

Christians, who are to show the relationship of Christ and the Church to the world, have the choice to cry, "You made your bed, now lie in it!" and ever remind their mates of their transgressions or mistakes, or they can say as Jesus, "Take up thy bed and walk. Thy sins be forgiven thee."

Henry Ward Beecher wrote, "'I can forgive, but I cannot forget,' is only another way of saying, 'I will not forgive.' Forgiveness ought to be like a canceled note—torn in two, and burned up, so that it never can be shown against one." [7]


## Allow Cooperation.

For a marriage to work, there must be a pulling together, working toward one cause. There is power in unity! Genesis 11:6 proves this: "And the Lord said, Behold, the people is one, and they have all one language; and this they begin to do: and now nothing will be restrained from them, which they have imagined to do." When people are united, they can accomplish most anything.

The old axiom, "United we stand, divided we fall," is still true today! Jesus said in Matthew 12:25, "Every kingdom divided against itself is brought to desolation; and every city or house divided against itself shall not stand." It is imperative that husband and wife stand together in goals, purpose and love, or their house will fall apart!

Make sure you both know what your goals are, and what you are agreed upon, so there is no confusion. Walter B. Knight tells the story about a well-groomed man who stood for several minutes watching a muscular delivery man heaving at trying to move a heavy box. It was almost as wide as the doorway through which he was trying to move it. The onlooker asked, "Would you like to have me help you?"

"Sure thing," said the man.

For two minutes the two men, on opposite ends of the box lifted, pulled and perspired. The box didn't move an inch. Finally, the volunteer helper straightened up and said, "I don't believe we can ever get it out!"

"Get it *out?*" the delivery man roared. "Why, you fool, I'm trying to get it *in!*"

Make sure both husband and wife know which way to push!

**Allow Faith.**

It is important for many reasons for faith to dominate your home. Medical doctor Andrew C. Ivy stated the following:

Religious attitudes of mind help keep men's bodies healthy. Attitudes such as love, faith, hope, unselfishness, forgiveness, tolerance, and a desire for justice and truth set the body at rest and strengthen it physically. Anti-religious attitudes such as hate, envy, jealousy, guilt, vanity, malice, vindictiveness and selfishness put a strain on the body and are conducive to the development of disease. [8]

Not only does faith leave you feeling better physically, but it also affects your mental health. Marriages that have the *climate* of faith permeating the atmosphere of the home leave everyone feeling refreshed, encouraged and looking upward. Faith begets faith. It is contagious. In the atmosphere of faith, things flourish, hope is renewed and people's spirits come alive.

Hebrews 11:6 states that it is impossible to please God without faith. If it is impossible to please God without faith, then it is impossible to please each other without it, because God is more merciful than human beings. As husband and wife start their married journey together on the sea of life, they need a good compass that will help chart their course and lead them to victory. There will be rocks in the sea, treacherous shores and hidden dangers that will lurk in the shadows of the night. Only the compass of faith will guide them through the darkness.

Walter B. Knight tells the story about a minister who was crossing the Atlantic on a freighter. The captain called his attention to two compasses. The lower compass was affected by the steel in the framework of the ship. "The pilot steers by the higher compass," said the captain.

"That's the way it should be as we steer our ship through life's stormy sea. The compass of feeling is affected by the changing winds of time and circumstances, and may dash us upon the rocks. The compass higher up—the compass of faith—points steadily to the changeless One—Jesus," answered the minister. [9]

This is exactly how husband and wife should steer their way through life—with the compass of faith.

"...prepare thee stuff for removing..."

Ezekiel 12:3

# 8

# REMOVE

DON ASLETT SAYS the following in his book, *Make Your House Do the Housework:*

> Before you pick up a hammer or draw up a single floor plan, there is one important thing you must remember: The first rule of housework is *prevent it.* Clutter is one of the greatest enemies of efficiency and stealers of time. Junk makes every job harder and makes cleaning take forever. Any project will be slowed, dampened, and diluted if you constantly have to fight your way to it through a mountain of clutter. First, remove the clutter. [1]

Just as removing clutter is important in housecleaning, so is it important in keeping a marriage *clean* from the debris of the accumulation of life. Old hurts, ugly spirits, grudges or anything that keeps the marriage from being built into something beautiful needs to be removed every so often. Take the time to remove the things that grate on the nerves of one another and the things that cause each other pain, which will eventually destroy the marriage.

**Remove Discord.**

"We have no more right to put our discordant states of mind into the lives of those around us and rob them of their sunshine and brightness than we have to enter their houses and steal their silverware." [2]

"If men [husband and wife] would consider not so much wherein they differ, as wherein they agree, there would be far less of uncharitableness and angry feeling in the world [marriage]." [3]

It is best not to say something that will wound and divide. President Calvin Coolidge once said, "I have never been hurt by anything I didn't say." [4] Note this other wise advice penned years ago: "The best time for you to hold your tongue is the time you feel you must say something or bust." [5]

Colossians 3:19 says, "Husbands, love your wives, and be not bitter against them." This means not using caustic, painful, stinging, distressing, piercingly harsh or cruel words. God knew the potential power that men possessed, and that they would be able to wound with words. Words can be like a hammer to the mind. "The pain of the mind is worse than the pain of the body." [6]

The friction of discord always grates on the nerves of a marriage!

**Remove Discourtesy**.

Learn to be courteous. Ralph Waldo Emerson once said, "Life is not so short but that there is always time for courtesy." [7]

The home is where you should be your kindest, most hospitable and best mannered. It should be your goal to be the same kind person all the time, so you never have to *put on*. Mrs. Arthur Sulzberger, of the newspaper dynasty, was bidding a granddaughter good-night one evening when the child remarked, "Mommy and Daddy are entertaining some very important people downstairs."

"You're right," agreed Mrs. Sulzberger. "But how did you know?"

"Just listen." advised her granddaughter. "Mommy is laughing at all of Daddy's jokes." [8]

"Don't flatter yourself that friendship authorizes you to say disagreeable things to your intimates. The nearer you come into relation with a person, the more necessary do tact and courtesy become." [9]

Courtesy can become instinctive in people if they consistently and intentionally work to cultivate courteous behavior. The opposite of courtesy is rudeness and thoughtlessness, and will tear down a marriage very quickly.

**Remove Irresponsibility.**

Winston Churchill once said, "Responsibility is the price of greatness." [10] Husbands and wives who want a great marriage will both learn to be responsible. Learning responsibility requires discipline.

Paul gives the key to success in I Corinthians 9:24-27. It reads as follows:

Know ye not that they which run in a race run all, but one receiveth the prize? So run, that ye may obtain. And every man that striveth for the mastery is temperate in all things. Now they do it to obtain a corruptible crown; but we an incorruptible. I therefore so run, not as uncertainly; so fight I, not as one that beateth the air: But I keep under my body, and bring it into subjection.

When athletes get ready for a race, the first thing they do is strip down and get rid of all the weights, those things that would hinder them from winning. Unused muscles must be developed and the body fine tuned for winning. The daily regime of working out and getting in shape requires discipline.

More important than just getting the body in shape, Paul says, is to get the inner man in shape. This requires reading the Word, prayer, meditation and fasting. As the sacrifice of physical food or other pleasures enables the athlete to become a winner, so it is in the spirit. When people sacrifice certain things that tend to make them spiritually sluggish, in order to receive spiritual food, they always grow and develop the inner disciplines of the soul. Their growth helps take away the weaknesses of the flesh and sloppy living.

A marriage is always strengthened as each partner works to remove an irresponsible attitude, for it is impossible to have a good marriage if both mates do not keep their word or do the things which spell success.

**Remove Debt**.

Someone once said, "Many marriages crack up when the installment collector cracks down." Robert J. Hastings wrote,

Money Management is not so much a technique as it is attitude. And when we talk about attitudes, we are dealing with emotions. Thus, money management is basically self-management or control of one's emotions. Unless one learns to control himself, he is no more likely to control his money than he is to discipline his habits, his time, or his temper. Undisciplined money usually spells undisciplined persons. [11]

The following comments about debt were made by well-known public figures:

*Ogden Nash:* "Some debts are fun when you are acquiring them, but none are fun when you set about retiring them." [12]

*Thomas Fuller:* "Debt is the worst poverty." [13]

*Ralph Waldo Emerson:* "A man in debt is so far a slave." [14]

*Thomas Jefferson:* "Never spend your money before you have it." [15]

*Publilius Syrus:* "Debt is the slavery of the free." [16]

*Samuel Johnson:* "Without economy none can be rich, and with it few will be poor." [17]

*Benjamin Franklin:* "Beware of little expenses, a small leak will sink a great ship." [18]

*Confucius:* "He who will not economize will have to agonize." [19]

If the above statements are true, which they are, then it is important to have a budget and to know where every penny of your money goes. If you will first pay God the ten percent tithe that belongs to Him, plus give offerings for His work, and live with self-control, you will begin to see a profit in your finances and your life. It is God's way. The Lord smiles upon a good steward.

Although the way people handle money is learned from the parents, bad habits can be broken. Thrift is not always an inherited quality, it is a habit that can be attained.

Someone once wrote the following about money: "Dug from the mountain, washed in the glen; servant am I or the master of men. Steal me—I curse you. Earn me—I bless you. Grasp me and hoard me, a fiend shall possess you; die for me; covet me; take me, angel or devil, I am what you make me—MONEY!" [20]

There needs to be thrift and a system of saving in every marriage, even if it is a very small amount. Benjamin Franklin said it well: "Let honesty and industry be thy constant companions, and spend one penny less than thy clear gains; then shall thy pocket begin to thrive; creditors will not insult, nor want oppress, nor hungerness bite, nor nakedness freeze thee." [21]

The Bible has the following things to say about the subject of money:

Proverbs 22:7: "The rich ruleth over the poor, and the borrower is servant to the lender."

Proverbs 10:4: "He becometh poor that dealeth with a slack hand; but the hand of the diligent maketh rich."

Malachi 3:8,10-11: "Will a man rob God? Yet ye have robbed me. But ye say, Wherein have we robbed thee? In tithes and offerings. Bring ye all the tithes into the storehouse, that there may be meat in mine house, and prove me now herewith, saith the Lord of hosts, if I will not open you the windows of heaven, and pour you out a blessing, that there shall not be room enough to receive it. And I will rebuke the devourer for your sakes."

Proverbs 6:6-11: "Go to the ant, thou sluggard: consider her ways, and be wise: Which having no guide, overseer, or ruler, Provideth her meat in the summer, and gathereth her food in the harvest. How long wilt thou sleep, O sluggard? when wilt thou arise out of thy sleep? Yet a little sleep, a little slumber, a little folding of the hands to sleep: So shall thy poverty come as one that travelleth, and thy want as an armed man."

In other words, you must have a plan and you must work your plan if you want to be successful in money matters.

## Remove Cynicism.

"A cynic can chill and dishearten with a single word," wrote Ralph Waldo Emerson. [22] There is nothing more disheartening than being around a cynical person. Henry Ward Beecher expresses why: "The cynic is one who never sees a good quality in a man, and never fails to see a bad one." [23]

Cynical people express their feelings in words, that is why it is important to be careful of your choice of words. One writer explained it like this: "The difference between the right word and the almost right word is the difference between lightning and the lightning bug." [24]

A cynic is one who finds fault and believes that human conduct is motivated wholly by self-interest. He is contemptuous and distrustful of human nature and motives. Often a cynical person will resort to sarcasm. Sarcasm is to speak with bitter remarks and express contempt in a sarcastic attitude. Thomas Carlyle did what every husband and wife need to do. He said, "Sarcasm is the language of the devil, for which reason I have long since as good as renounced it." [25]

## Remove Character Flaws.

Someone once said, "The difficulty with marriage is that we fall in love with a personality, but must live with a character." [26]

It is the responsibility of both husband and wife to work on deleting character flaws. The question is asked, "How?" Let the following paragraph help you understand how this is possible:

Our lives are the strongest part of us—or the weakest. A man knows the least of the influence of his own life. Life is not mere length of time, but the daily web of character we unconsciously weave. Our thoughts, imaginations, purposes, motives, love, will, are the under threads: our words, tone of voice, looks, acts, habits are the upper threads; and the passing moment is the shuttle swiftly, ceaselessly, relentlessly, weaving those threads into a web, and that web is life. It is woven, not by our wishing, or willing, but irresistibly, unavoidably, woven by what we are, moment by moment, hour after hour. [27]

If you can control a minute, then you can control two minutes. If you can control two minutes, you can control sixty minutes. Live each minute as if it were your last on earth, for each moment has destiny attached to it. Each minute determines what you are becoming. The crux of the matter is: work at removing that which makes you ugly, bitter or flawed inside.

## Remove Lust or Potential Unfaithfulness.

Christian Nestell Bovee wrote, "The body of a sensualist is the coffin of a dead soul." [28] Who wants to live in a coffin? We declare to all who read this book: Keep your eyes on your mate! Have eyes only for one another. Sometimes the grass appears to be greener on the other side of the fence, but it is the same grass. The grass is not greener on the other side of the fence or the other side of the world. The grass is green right in your own backyard. If not, put some water of love on it and work with it and you can produce the finest grass around. If you experience a temporary romantic feeling towards someone else, have sense enough to put it aside and not dwell on it. Pull the reigns tight on your emotions and call a halt to a dangerous "biological pull" from the opposite sex that would threaten your marriage. You already have what you need. Sometimes you just have to work at discovering it, as the following story depicts.

There was once a Persian man by the name of Ali Hafed who owned a very large farm. He had orchards, fields of grain, gardens and money and was a very contented, wealthy man. One day he was visited by a priest who was considered to be a wise man of the East. He sat down by the fire and told the farmer how this world was made and how diamonds were made.

Said the old priest, "A diamond is a congealed drop of sunlight." He then told Ali that if he had one diamond the size of his thumb he could purchase the county, and if he had a mine of diamonds he could place his children upon thrones through the influence of great wealth.

Later that night Ali Hafed went to bed a poor man. He had not lost anything, but he was poor because he was discontented, and discontented because he feared he was poor. He thought, "I want a mine of diamonds," and he lay awake all night thinking about it.

The next morning he sought out the old priest and asked him how he could find diamonds. The priest told him that if he could find a river that runs through white sands he would find diamonds. Ali said, "I don't believe there is such a river."

The priest said, "Oh yes, there are plenty of them. All you have to do is go and find them."

So Ali sold his farm, collected his money, left his family in charge of a neighbor, and went in search of diamonds. He wandered around Palestine, then journeyed on into Europe until his money was gone. When he was in rags, wretchedness and poverty, he stood on the shore of the bay at Barcelona, Spain, when a great tidal wave came rolling in between the pillars of Hercules, and the poor, afflicted, suffering man could not resist the terrible temptation to cast himself into that incoming tide. He sank beneath its foaming crest, gone forever.

Meanwhile back at the farm, the man who had purchased Ali's farm went into the garden one day to water his camel at the shallow water of the garden brook. He noticed a curious flash of light from the white sands of the stream. He pulled out a black stone having an eye of light reflecting all the hues of the rainbow. He took the pebble into the house and put it on the fireplace mantel and forgot all about it.

Until one day the old priest came by to visit him. The moment he opened the drawing room door he saw that flash of light on the mantel, and he rushed over to it and shouted, "Here is a diamond! Has Ali Hafed returned?"

"Oh no, Ali has not returned, and that is not a diamond. That is nothing but a stone we found right here in our own garden."

But the priest said, "I tell you that is a diamond. I know one when I see it."

Together the farmer and the priest rushed out into that old garden and stirred up the white sands with their fingers and lo! there came up other more beautiful and valuable gems than the first. This was how the diamond mine of Golconda, the most magnificent diamond mine in all the history of mankind, was found. As the priest swung his hat, he said to the farmer, "Had Ali Hafed remained at home and dug in his own cellar, or underneath his own wheat fields, or in his own garden, instead of searching around the world, he would have had acres of diamonds."

How true it is. Every man or woman has treasure right in their own home, within their own marriage, but sometimes it is hidden underneath a dark, crusty veneer. Work at removing that which hides the *diamond* and remember that what you need is in your own corporation of marriage. It might need some help and rejuvenation, but it is there. It is up to you to work at finding it and making it so.

**Remove Gossip**.

It is imperative that you ban hurtful gossip from your home, for in time gossip will ruin a home. Whatever you give out comes back to you. The negative vibes you send forth in evil reports and slander will turn and attach themselves to your spirit.

The following verse is taken from some material we read years ago—just a little food for thought:

Little people talk about other people.
Common people talk about things.
Great people talk about ideas and dreams.

Seek to talk about things which uplift and inspire.

**Remove Bad Habits**.

From the Talmud comes the following quote: "A *bad habit* is first a *caller*, then a *guest*, and at last a *master*." [29]

Samuel Johnson said it like this: "The chains of habit are generally too small to be felt until they are too strong to be broken. Habits are at first cobwebs—at last cables." [30]

Another writer explained it this way: "Habits, though in their commencement like the filmy line of a spider, trembling at every breeze, may, in the end, prove as links of tempered steel." [31]

Habits may be strong, but with God all things are possible to him that believes. God's spirit is so powerful, He can help you break any habit.

"Seek ye out of the book of the Lord, and read."

Isaiah 34:16

#

ANDRE MAUROIS WISELY said, "A successful marriage is an edifice that must be rebuilt every day." [1]

Frank Crane defined the building of a marriage in the following words:

> The walls of a house are not built of wood, brick or stone, but of truth and loyalty. Unpleasant sounds, the friction of living, the clash of personalities, are not deadened by Persian rugs or polished floors, but by conciliation, concession, and self-control....The house is not a structure where bodies meet, but a hearthstone upon which flames mingle, separate flames of souls, which, the more perfectly they unite, the more clearly they shine and the straighter they rise toward heaven. [2]

Do not wait until there is *big* trouble with your edifice, but take inventory daily of the status of your marital relationship you are building. Samuel Smiles pinpointed the cause of bad luck. He said, "It will generally be found that men [women] who are constantly lamenting their ill luck are only reaping the consequences of their own neglect, mismanagement, and improvidence, or want of application." [3]

Another writer likened life to a building. We say his explanation can apply to a marriage. He wrote:

Life [marriage] is a building. It rises slowly day by day, through the years. Every new lesson we learn lays a block on the edifice which is rising silently within us. Every experience, every touch of another life on ours, every influence that impresses us, every book we read, every conversation we have, every act of our commonest days, add something to the invisible building. [4]

In order to build a beautiful edifice of marriage, there must be some good material put into the framework. You are not building a house of wood, stone and brick, but you are building a structure that involves the heart, mind, soul and spirit; therefore, you must keep them inspired and challenged. How do you do that? You introduce new ideas into your mind. You are or become what you read! You might ask, "How can reading help me to have a good marriage?" Let us seek to answer that question in this important chapter.

The printed page is powerful. Joseph Addison said, "Reading is to the mind what exercise is to the body." [5] Without exercise the body will slowly become weak, flabby and sluggish; eventually it will die. Without positive stimulation of the mind through reading the Bible and good books, the same thing will happen to the mind. People can become prisoners in their mind. The following men and women spoke of the power of the printed page:

*Benjamin Franklin*: "Give me 26 lead soldiers, and I'll conquer the world, for the pen is mightier than the sword." [6]

*Professor T.C. McGrew*: "The printed word is in the end the great temporal power in the world. The missiles of dictators can shatter cities thousands of miles away, but the printing press can shatter an empire at the range of a thousand years." [7]

*G.W. Curtis*: "Books are the ever-burning lamps of accumulated wisdom." [8]

*Emile Poulsson*:

Books are keys to wisdom's treasure
Books are gates to lands of pleasure;
Books are paths that upward lead;
Books are friends, Come, let us read. [9]

*Christopher Morley*: "When you sell a man a book you don't sell him just twelve ounces of paper and ink and glue—you sell him a whole new life." [10]

*Sydney Smith*: "We should accustom the mind to keep the best company by introducing it only to the best books." [11]

*Charles Kingsley*:

Except a living man there is nothing more wonderful than a book! A message to us from…human souls we never saw, who lived, perhaps, thousands of miles away. And yet these, in those little sheets of paper, speak to us, arouse us, terrify us, teach us, comfort us, open their hearts to us…. [12]

Many times marital problems stem from ignorance. When the mind constantly counsels itself over and over with stale and unsuccessful ideas, those ideas gradually develop into negative thought patterns. It is necessary to read and expand the mind with new inspirational thoughts which affect behavior. "For as he thinketh in his heart, so is he" (Proverbs 23:7). Shakespeare penned the words, "'Tis the mind that makes the body rich." [13]

Horace Mann wrote, "There is nothing so costly as ignorance." [14] Books are one of the best ways to undo this ignorance, but be careful of what you read. Be sure that any book you read corresponds with the Bible in its thoughts and principles; if not, throw it away.

Tyron Edwards said, "We should be as careful of the books we read, as of the company we keep. The dead very often have more power than the living." [15]

Not only do you need to be choosy about what is allowed to influence your mind, but after learning from the printed page, it is just as important to apply what is learned. Saadia said, "He who learns and makes no use of his learning is a beast of burden with a load of books." [16]

The opportunity to learn is all around us. We are surrounded by a wealth of knowledge, but what we do with it is up to us. The following poem says it well:

"Isn't It Strange?"

Isn't it strange
That princes and kings,
And clowns that caper
In sawdust rings,
And common people
Like you and me
Are builders of eternity?

Each is given a bag of tools,
A shapeless mass,
A book of rules;
And each must make–
Ere life is flown–
A stumbling block
Or a steppingstone.

*R. L. Sharpe* [17]

A want for good books should be our desire, as it was for Henry Van Dyke, who wrote,

I want the books that help me out of the vacancy and despair of a frivolous mind, out of the tangle and confusion of a society that is buried in bric-a-brac, out of the meanness of unfeeling mockery and the heaviness of incessant mirth, into a loftier and serener region, where, through the clear air of serious thoughts, I can learn to look soberly and bravely upon the mingled misery and splendor of human existence, and then go down with a cheerful courage to play a man's part in the life which Christ has forever ennobled by His Divine Presence. [18]

"But it is good to be zealously affected always in a good thing."

Galatians 4:18

# INFLUENCE

WORDS WRITTEN OVER 75 years ago by Rev. J.R. Miller appeared in the book *Quests and Conquests*. These words simmer with inspiration. They are not just an ideal, but the truth they portray is reachable through Christ.

Every influence of the word of Christ is toward beauty and joy. Some homes have always a somber air. Some people's religion seems to make them severe and ungentle. But that is not the Christ way. The religion which the word of Christ inspires is sunny and full of song. Some one writes, "We want a religion that softens the step, turns the voice to melody, fills the eye with sunshine, and checks the impatient exclamation and harsh rebuke, a religion that is polite to all, deferential to superiors, considerate to friends; a religion that goes into the family and keeps the husband from being cross when dinner is late, that keeps the wife from fretting when the husband tracks the only washed floor with his soiled boots, and makes the husband mindful of the doormat; that keeps the mother patient when the baby is cross, and amuses the children as well as instructs them; that projects the honeymoon into the harvest moon, and makes the happy home like the Eastern fig-tree, bearing on its bosom at once the tender blossoms and the glory of the ripening fruit." [1]

Husband and wife are two people living together under the same roof. Their attitudes and character influence and affect one another. It is important to earnestly seek to influence each other for good. Lillian Whiting stated it well: "The fine art of living is to draw from each person his best."

One writer once wrote,

Fortunate, indeed, the community that has a few individuals who go through life curing sorrows, allaying discontents, healing enmities, sweetening bitter fountains, scattering happiness and good-will. One such nature can influence an entire community, just as one flower will crowd a room with sweet odors. [2]

In a cemetery a little white stone marked the grave of a dear little girl, and on the stone were chiseled these words—"A child of who her playmates said, 'It was easier to be good when she was with us'—one of the most beautiful epitaphs ever heard of." [3]

When things go wrong, it is easy to sink into the doldrums of boredom and self-pity. Instead get your mind off yourself and fill it with inspiration. Seek to bring pizzazz, good character, life and class to your marriage. Influence your partner with knowledge, good attitudes and optimism.

You are the engineer of your thoughts and actions. Those thoughts not only affect the home, but they reach out into your community, church and everything that you touch. "Thought is the soul's chariot. The thoughtless man doesn't get his soul any-where." [4] Thoughts can also be a person's private hell. Be careful of your thoughts, for you are what you think about all day long.

It is important to bring culture into each other's life. Culture should enrich your life. One writer explained what real culture was: "Real culture is found in wealth of thought, wealth of ap-preciation, wealth of sympathy, all expressed in daily ministries of kindness." [5]

*Webster's Dictionary* defines *culture* as "cultivation." It is "the act of developing by education, discipline and training." Culture is "enlightenment and refinement of taste acquired by intellectual means."

Margaret Fuller said it well: "A house is not a home unless it contains food and fire for the mind as well as the body." [6]

The following people concurred with Margaret Fuller and be-lieved that acquiring culture was important:

*Jesse Bennett:* "The acquiring of culture is the development of an avid hunger for knowledge and beauty." [7]

*Henry Ward Beecher:* "That is true culture which helps us to work for the social betterment of all." [8]

*W. Somerset Maugham:* "The end of culture is right living." [9]

The following things help to shape your home and bring culture into it:

## Music

Music can speak messages that cannot be spoken with words. Aldous Husley said, "That which comes nearest to expressing the inexpressible is music," [10] while Hans Christian Anderson said it this way: "Where words fail, music speaks." [11]

It is important to listen to only that which makes the soul grow bigger, that which is uplifting, inspiring and that ministers. Sara Teasdale believed that music could touch chords deep within the heart, as shown in the following poem:

As they sang—
Of what I know not, but the music touched
Each chord of being—I felt my secret life
Stand open to it as the parched earth yawns
To drink the summer rain; and at the call
Of those refreshing waters, all my thoughts

Stir from their dark and secret depths, and burst
Into sweet, odorous flowers, and from their wells
Deep calls to deep and all the mystery
Of all that is, is laid open. [12]

Not only does music enrich the heart, but it also stirs the passions, as Henri-Frederic Amiel once wrote:

This morning the music of a brass band which had stopped under my windows moved me almost to tears. It exercised an indefinable, nostalgic power over me; it set the dreaming of another world, of infinite passion and supreme happiness. Such impressions are the echoes of Paradise in the soul; memories of ideal spheres, whose sad sweetness ravishes and intoxicates the heart. [13]

Men of renown have said the following about music and its influence:

*Plato*: "Music is to the soul what air is to the body." [14]

*Goethe*: "Every day one should hear a little music, read a good poem, and gaze upon a fine picture." [15]

*Napoleon Bonaparte*: "Of all the liberal arts, music has the greatest influence over the passions." [16]

*Gladstone*: "Music is one of the most forcible instruments for arousing and for governing the mind and the spirit of man." [17]

*Theodore Roosevelt*: "Let the love of literature...and above all, music, enter your lives." [18]

*Dr. Charles W. Eliot, president emeritus of Harvard*: "Music, rightly taught, is the best mind trainer in our curriculum." [19]

*Shakespeare*: "The man who hath not music in his soul, nor is moved with concord of sweet sounds, is fit for treasons, stratagems, and spoils, let no man trust him." [20]

*Martin Luther*:

Music is a fair and lovely gift of God which has often wakened and moved me to the joy of preaching....Next after theology, I give to music the highest place and the greatest honor....My heart bubbles up and overflows in response to music, which has so often refreshed me and delivered me from dire plagues. [21]

## Books and Literature

We will not belabor this point as it has already been covered in Chapter 9, however, a few additional comments are in order.

Joseph Addison said it well: "Reading is to the mind what exercise is to the body." [22]

It does not require much to read a good book, as Mary Worley Montagu so ably stated: "No entertainment is so cheap as reading, nor any pleasure so lasting." [23]

Scanning is for the newspaper, but one should practice con-centration when reading worthwhile literature. A pencil should always be at hand. Impressive words, lines and thoughts should be underlined. When you read something that greatly inspires you, copy it, rewrite, it, memorize it, and saturate your soul with it.

"Perhaps no other things have such power to lift the poor out of poverty, the wretched out of misery, to make the burden bearer forget his burden, the sick his suffering, as books." [24]

## Friends

Avoid those who draw you away from each other or cause a wedge in your family. Do not choose the flirts, the gossips and the cheaters to be your bosom friends, for their spirit will seep into your relationship. The old adage is still true, "If you trot with the skunk, you will carry his smell." The people you surround yourself with definitely have an influence on your marriage.

George Washington said, "Associate yourself with men of good quality if you esteem your own reputation; for 'tis better to be alone than in bad company." [25]

Avoid friends who leave you feeling dirty or down in your spirit. Seek out those who can be an inspiration to your marriage or that cause you to stretch and reach for greater things. You can be kind to everyone, but those you run with should be in search of excellence also.

Choosing friends is an important action. Lillian Whiting said it so well, "Friendship is in itself as fine an act as is music, or painting, or sculpture." Your friends definitely affect the quality of life you will have.

The following essay expresses what a true friend should be:

"I Love You"

I love you not only for what you are but for what I am when I'm with you;

I love you not only for what you have made of yourself but what you are making of me.

I love you for putting your hand into my heaped up heart and passing over all the foolish weak things you can't help dimly seeing there, and drawing out in the light all the beautiful belongings that no one else had looked quite far enough to find.

I love you because you are helping me to make of the lumber of my life not a tavern but a temple, out of the work of my every day life not a reproach but a song;

I love you because you have done more than any creed could have done to make me good and more than any fate could have done to make me happy;

You have done it without a touch, without a word, without a sigh;

You have done it by being yourself.

Perhaps that is what being a friend means, after all. [26]

## Entertainment

That which you do for fun and relaxation should be stimulating in the sense that it revives you from a weary or tired state, but it should also be clean, inspirational and enriching.

Do not do anything that you would not want to be doing if Jesus were present or if the trumpet sounded for the great "catching away." Life is too short to live in the gray areas. There is too much good to choose from, so why sift through the garbage? Leave the trash at the dump where it belongs and let the rats and pests enjoy it. But as for you, you must make a decision to engage in only that which leaves you feeling refreshed, inspired and clean. Your bodies are temples of the *holy* God and your marriage is the *temple* of your love. God should feel comfortable dwelling in both of them.

Whatever you partake of will either degrade or enhance your relationship with each other and also with God, so choose well.

## Words

Edwin Arnold wrote, "Govern the lips as if they were palace doors, the king within." [27] There has been much said in this book about words, but because their influence is so powerful, they must once more be brought to the attention of the reader.

In *Quests & Conquests* was found the following resolve, which would be a good guiding star for all marriages:

"My High Resolve—the Ministry of Words"

What I am gives color and power to what I say. I shall be peaceful and gentle in all my conversations. I resolve never to scold or be impatient. I shall cultivate a well-poised voice.

I shall cultivate the use of the language. I shall select my words as I would flowers for a friend. Coarse, ugly language, slovenly thrown together, I shall weed out. These mar conversation and clog the flow of helpful language.

I shall never speak carelessly to children nor before them. I shall purpose to be a model in the art of using words.

The wealth of experience, sure to be mine as I climb the heights of growth and service, will afford me inspiring subjects for conversation.

I shall seek to enrichen other lives by telling of my encouragements, of my inspirations, of gems of literature that have helped me, of songs that have cheered me, of blessings that have comforted me.

Nothing so enrichens language like the touches of the spiritual forces. The very life of God flows out through our language when we are in tune with Him. There is something of the touch of the life of God that mellows and in a beautiful way gives meaning to our words so that they melt into the very hearts of those we are with. Wisdom is given us to say just the right thing at the strategic time so that life building investments are made of life long value. [28]

Stanford wrote,

Thoughts and words travel...They do not travel like an individual, but breathe your spiritual life into the atmosphere as you do your breath, and some one else breathes it in. Those not present still perceive it, for it permeates space, and all live in it and receive from it according to their unfoldment. [29]

"And he declared unto you his covenant, which he commanded you to perform."

Deuteronomy 4:13

# CT

YOU ARE ON stage. *Your Marriage* is the name of the play. Each day makes up the plot. You and your husband are the main actors. It is all in there: joy, tears, sorrow, happiness, disappointments, hurts, resentments, laughter, trials, ecstasy, memories and hundreds of other things.

God has a plan and writes the guidelines for the script for each life, but many times the actors embellish it, change it, or interpret it differently than how He planned it to be. Along with the written script, He also gives freedom of thought and allows each actor to write portions of the script. An unknown author said it well in the following verse:

You are writing a gospel,

A chapter each day;
By deeds that you do;
By words that you say;
Men read what you write,
Whether faulty or true.
Say, what is the gospel
According to you? [1]

No one can act yesterday, for yesterday is gone. Neither can anyone act tomorrow, for tomorrow is not here. The only time anyone can act is "Today," so do it well!

In order to polish the Act, thought must be given to the following things:

## Dress

One anonymous writer wrote, "The body is the shell of the soul, and dress the husk of that shell; but the husk often tells what the kernel is." [2]

Have you ever worked hard all day and felt dirty, rumpled and tired, then went in, took a bath, put on new clothes and felt a whole lot better? We concur with Ella Wheeler Wilcox who expressed this transformation as follows: "There is new strength, repose of mind, and inspiration in fresh apparel." [3]

It is important for husbands to keep a sparkle in their eyes, a kind smile, a masculine manner and a self-controlled spirit. But it is also important to dress in clean, coordinated clothes. A man of excellence will want his wife to say with pride, "There goes my man! Look at him. Isn't he handsome!" Dirty, rumpled clothes subtract from the appearance.

Clothes that are nice and clean impress people as to the character of the individual. Coleman Cox said it well: "Keeping your clothes well pressed will keep you from looking hard pressed." [4]

The Bible says in Psalm 45:13 that "The king's daughter is all glorious within: her clothing is of wrought gold." It is important for wives to keep a sparkle in their eyes, a warm smile, a radiant, fresh, lady-like manner and a gentle, peaceful spirit, but it is also important to dress attractively. Their clean, modest, and attractive clothes will portray that they are women of quality and worth. The husband should look at the wife and say with pride, "That's my woman. She's got *class*."

**Attitudes**

Hugh Downs said, "A happy person is not a person in a certain set of circumstances, but rather a person with a certain set of attitudes." [5] He brought up a good point: attitudes. An attitude is a posture or position indicating action, feeling or mood. A feeling is an emotional state. A mood is a particular state of mind showing the feeling of the heart.

Era Easley writes the following:

Psychologists have convinced us that the emotions play a great part in determining the trend of our actions. The emotions, rather than the intellect, determine our character. How human beings conduct themselves in the absence of restraint depends upon their appetites, their preferences for good or for evil, for the beautiful or for the unlovely, for the higher or for the lower levels of life. Each individual reacts to his own desires. His decisions are controlled by his feelings. Whether he is to be a law-abiding citizen or a menace to society depends upon the sum total of his appetites, rather than upon his reasoning power. The controlling elements in his character are emotional and spiritual rather than intellectual. [6]

Attitudes will definitely determine the way a person acts or reacts in a marriage relationship.

## Character

The word *act* is an integral part of character. Character is what you are. It is the way you act in the dark when no one is watching you. It has much to do with how people think about you. Proverbs 22:1 says, "A good name is rather to be chosen than great riches, and loving favour rather than silver and gold." All the gold and wealth of the earth is not worth losing a good name.

Character does not fall out of the air. It is made, and many times there is a struggle. George Dana Boardman wrote, "Let us not say, Every man is the architect of his own fortune; but let us say, Every man is the architect of his own character." [7]

Character is made and attained by the choices that are made. One writer wrote, "Our character is but the stamp on our souls of the free choices of good and evil we have made through life." [8] Abraham Lincoln said, "Character is like a tree and reputation is like the shadow. The shadow is what we think of it; the tree is the real thing." [9]

## Conversation

What you are gives color and power to what you say. Cultivate the use of fine language. Select your words as you would choose flowers for a friend. Common gossip is a symptom of an empty mind. Talking about other's faults and shortcomings is unprofitable and very displeasing to God. Shine in your conversation by always speaking kindly and gently of all of whom you speak at all. *Remember*: intercession in prayer is wonderful for correcting evil; gossip is not.

James asks the question, "Who is a wise man and endued with knowledge among you? Let him show out of a good conversation his works with meekness of wisdom" (James 3:13).

## POINTS TO PONDER FOR THOSE INVOLVED IN THE ACT OF MARRIAGE

*For the Wife:*

Jeremy Taylor described a good wife. He wrote,

A good wife is Heaven's last best gift to man—his gem of many virtues, his chest of jewels; her voice is sweet music, her smiles his brightest day, her kiss the guardian of his innocence, her arms the bounds of his safety, her industry his surest wealth, her economy his safest steward, her lips his faithful counselor, her bosom the softest pillow of his cares. [10]

- Seek to be the unforgettable woman in your husband's life.
- Be a sweetheart, vibrant and alive.
- Do not be lazy.
- Keep yourself lovable.
- Fix your husband nutritious meals.
- Do not fill your husband's mind with gossip.
- Develop into a good conversationalist. Stay informed.
- Make your husband secretly glad he is married to you.
- Learn to laugh in the rain; don't grumble.
- Feed your husband's ego.
- Learn to overlook his faults.
- Always be loyal.
- Become a person your husband likes to be with.

- Keep a clean, orderly house.

A Chinese Proverb says, "A hundred men may make an encampment, but it takes a woman to make a home." [11]

*For the Husband:*

- Be the unforgettable man in your wife's mind.
- Be a sweetheart, vibrant and alive.
- Do not be lazy.
- Keep yourself clean and attractive.
- Send your wife flowers.
- Share inspirational conversation with your wife. Do not clam up.
- Make your wife secretly glad she is married to you.
- Do not be a grouch!
- Learn to overlook your wife's faults.
- Always be loyal.
- Become the kind of person your wife enjoys being with.
- Let your home become your sanctuary.

Henry Ward Beecher wrote, "It is very dangerous for any man to find any spot on this broad globe that is sweeter to him than his home." [12]

"Give, and it shall be given unto you; good measure, pressed down, and shaken together, and running over, shall men give unto your bosom. For with the same measure that ye mete withal it shall be measured to you again."

Luke 6:38

# IVE

A SPRINGFIELD NEIGHBOR was drawn to his door one day by the crying of children. When he got there, he saw Abraham Lincoln passing by with his two sons, both crying lustily. "What is the matter with the boys?" asked the man.

"Just what is the matter with the whole world!" answered Lincoln. "I have three walnuts and each boy wants two."

Many times everyone is reaching and grabbing, but few are giving. True happiness comes when the covetous fist is opened and shared cheerfully with someone. Miserliness is misery. Not only is the miser miserable, but those in need are miserable. The misery could be alleviated if the one who had it to give would just give.

Marriage, as stated earlier, is an investment. Begin with the first day to seek to give your best to this union. Do not wait until there is trouble or when you are older. Percy Johnston said it this way: "It is the height of absurdity to sow little but weeds in the first half of one's lifetime and expect to harvest a valuable crop in the second half." [1]

If you want a rich marriage, begin to give freely to one another. "Not he who has much is rich, but he who gives much." [2]

In the area of giving certain things need to be considered which are listed below:

**Give space**.

Someone expressed well the difference between loneliness and solitude: "Language has created the word loneliness to express the pain of being alone, and the word solitude to express the glory of being alone." [3]

Everyone needs to have their alone time. When it comes that time for your mate, back off and do everything in your power to make it happen. Do it even if it means that the one who needs it can be undisturbed for several hours in a certain part of the house. There are times when the soul must catch up with the body and this can only happen in quietness and solitude.

Jesus, who knew the pressure and demands of the crowds, went alone into the mountains to pray. He had to get away from it all.

A word of warning: If each mate needs too much space too often, then there is a problem that needs to be examined.

**Give affection.**

Dr. Willard F. Harley, Jr., author of the book, *His Needs, Her Needs,* says,

Affection is the *environment* of the marriage while sex is an *event.* Affection is a way of life, a canopy that covers and protects a marriage. It's a direct and convincing expression of love that gives the event of sex a more appropriate context. [4]

He further states,

Some women will have sex with their husbands just for the affection they receive while making love, but it tends to leave them resentful and bitter. As soon as sex is over, their husbands go back to their unaffectionate ways, leaving their wives feeling unloved. They feel that all their husbands want is sex, and they don't really care about them in any other way....A woman's need for affection is probably her deepest emotional need...but her husband has an equally deep need for sex. To the typical man, sex is like air or water. He can't do without it very well...[Frustration] can be avoided if husbands learn to be more affectionate and wives respond with more eagerness to make love. [5]

**Give your mind, body and heart to your time of sexual enjoyment.**

Distractions, worry, stress and previous arguments can destroy the pleasure of sex. Learn the following twelve words which will help keep intimacy in marriage:

*I was wrong.*
*I am sorry.*
*Please, forgive me.*
*I love you.*

When forgiven, then seek to improve or change yourself. Someone once said, "The biggest room in the world is the room for improvement."

When life gets rushed, kids come along and everything seems like work, work, work, then it is essential for time to be set aside for intimacy, to harness the mind. You must get your minds off the bills, kids, diapers, responsibilities and other preoccupations, and zero in on what you are doing. Dream that you are making love on the beach by the ocean or on some secluded island. The wife can do the things that help create a conducive atmosphere for love: put on romantic music, light scented candles, bathe, use perfume or even fantasize that your prince is coming to sweep you off your feet and take you into the land of love.

God instituted marriage and intimacy. He ordained that man and woman would be joined together not only in spirit, but also to be passionately joined together and become one flesh through the sexual act.

Sex is honorable in marriage, dishonorable out of marriage. Hebrews 13:4 says, "Marriage is honorable in all, and the bed undefiled: but whoremongers and adulterers God will judge."

It is God's will that the husband be ravished with his wife's love. Proverbs 5:18,19 says, "Let thy fountain be blessed: and rejoice with the wife of thy youth. Let her be as the loving hind and pleasant roe; let her breasts satisfy thee at all times; and be thou ravished always with her love." *Ravish* means "to be transported with by the emotion of joy or delight."

Sex should be an exquisite delight as described in Song of Solomon 1:2,13; 4:11:

Let him kiss me with the kisses of his mouth: for thy love is better than wine. A bundle of myrrh is my well-beloved unto me; he shall lie all night betwixt my breasts. Thy lips, O my spouse, drop as the honeycomb: honey and milk are under thy tongue: and the smell of thy garments is like the smell of Lebanon.

Solomon describes the wife: "Thy navel is like a round goblet, which wanteth not liquor: thy belly is like an heap of wheat set about with lilies. Thy two breasts are like two young roes that are twins. How fair and how pleasant art thou, O love, for delights!" (Song of Solomon 7:2-3,6).

It is important for the husband and wife to both feel fulfilled and enjoy the pleasures of intimate love. Dr. G. Lombard Kelly, Professor of Anatomy at the University of Georgia, wrote the following in the book *Successful Marriage*:

Men and women have both been supplied with organs intended to make the marital relation mutually enjoyable. Especially sensitive microscopic nerve endings are present in the head of the penis and of the clitoris, and in the areas near these centers. Proper stimulation of these end organs under optimum conditions will result in that intense consummation of love, the climax of sexual feeling technically known as the orgasm...It is certainly not too much to ask that the bridegroom be the personification of tenderness. The bride should be courted and petted to the state of active passion...Meanwhile the husband searches and finds out what counts with her. She wants darkness or dim illumination, where he likes light. She rouses to endearments in the beginning of the caresses but must have silence absolute to concentrate on climax...A bridegroom who is selfish and cares only for his own satisfaction will certainly offend and disappoint a sensitive bride. If the woman is not quite apt and does not reach climax easily she may remain in an unsatisfied state, with a resultant congestion of her generative organs and an unrelieved nervous tension. If this one-sided kind of marital act is persisted in, the wife may tire of the disappointments and the nervous tension and turn against the act entirely. In short, the husband who does not take the necessary steps to make his relations with his wife mutually enjoyable and satisfactory may eventually ruin his marriage. [6]

It would appear that Dr. Kelly puts more blame on the man than the woman if there is not sexual enjoyment. Dr. O. Spurgeon English, Professor of Psychiatry at Temple University School of Medicine, Philadelphia, wrote the following in *Successful Marriage*:

We have the woman complaining that her husband never shows any interest in her or any tenderness toward her unless he desires sexual relations. He is unappreciative of her daily activities. When he does desire sexual relations he does not take time enough to excite her through caresses, kisses, and endearments. When intercourse begins he is not enough interested in...bringing his wife to orgasm, or in his verbal appreciation of her as a love partner to make her happy.

The man in turn complains that his wife is never interested in sex relations, or can't be made interested often enough, or is not appreciative enough of his advances. Or in sex relations she is physically inactive, emotionally unresponsive, takes too long to come to orgasm...She may even be critical of him as "lustful," or "lacking the proper appreciation of her" in wanting to have intercourse with her. [7]

Dr. English also shares the following report:

Dr. Kinsey's studies have pointed up some definite differences in the personality make-up of men and women. For instance, while practically all men are sexually aroused by the female body dressed or undressed, very few women are aroused sexually by sight of the male body clothed or unclothed. Similarly, men respond to pictures, stories, and exotic clothing, while women seem to respond only somewhat to a romantic movie [novel], chivalrous attention, and even to touch itself...He [husband] should understand additionally that kissing, caressing, and sex play should be used to arouse his wife to the point of sexual excitement and that this will make sex relations more enjoyable. He should not ignore or neglect this throughout his marriage. [8]

The professional comments of Dr. Kelly and Dr. English prove that a woman needs to feel loved and caressed before enjoying sexual intimacy. Nathaniel Hawthrone wrote, "Caresses, expressions of one sort or another, are necessary to the life of the affections as leaves are to the life of a tree." [9]

Washington Irving says, "A woman's life is a history of the affections." [10]

**Give love**.

This is for both husband and wife. Ephesians 5:33 states, "Nevertheless let every one of you in particular so love his wife even as himself." William Lyon Phelps said it like this:

However important sex instruction may be to marriage, there is one thing more important—*character*. Two people unselfish and considerate, tactful and warmhearted, and salted with humor, who are in love, have the most essential of all qualifications for a successful marriage—they have character. [11]

Paul called it the fruit of the spirit. Galatians 5:22-23 names the qualities that define love: "But the fruit of the Spirit is love, joy, peace, longsuffering, gentleness, goodness, faith, meekness, temperance...."

Colossians 3:12-14 emphasizes the importance of making love an integral part of life.

Put on therefore, as the elect of God, holy and beloved, bowels of mercies, kindness, humbleness of mind, meekness, longsuffering; forbearing one another, and forgiving one another, if any man have a quarrel against any: even as Christ forgave you, so also do ye. And above all these things put on charity, which is the bond of perfectness.

The Spirit understood man's sinful nature and inherent weaknesses; that is why Paul was inspired to write the words "Put on" in verse 12. Colossians 3:8 emphatically states that old spirits and attitudes need to be shed, so there can be a putting on of new ones. The spirits of Christ that husband and wife are to *put on* are as follows:

1. Bowels of mercies.
2. Kindness.
3. Humbleness of mind.
4. Meekness.
5. Longsuffering.
6. Forbearing one another.
7. Forgiving one another.

Paul ends the instructions by saying, "And above all these things put on charity, which is the bond of perfectness" (Colossians 3:14).

Let us examine briefly points 1 through 7 above.

*Bowels* in this sense means the seat of pity or kindness, tenderness and compassion. The interior of the soul and heart are to be filled with *mercies*. Note the plural: one show of mercy is not enough. *Mercy* means "compassionate treatment of an offender, the disposition to exercise compassion or forgiveness and the willingness to spare or to help."

*Kindness* is the state of being kind. *Kind* means "to show graciousness, tenderness or compassion." It is characterized by goodness or benevolence.

*Humbleness* is a lacking of pride or self-sufficiency, a mildness of temper, and unassuming.

*Meekness* is mild of temper, patient under injuries, gentle and kind.

*Longsuffering* means "to have long and patient endurance of offense."

*Forbear* means "to be patient and endure." It means "to refrain, restrain, hold back or control oneself."

*Forgive* means "to give up claim to requital from an offender, to pardon an enemy, or to remit the penalty of; as, to forgive a wrong."

No one is born with all of these attributes. They are goals to work toward. These qualities are drenched with self-discipline and self-control, and attained through Christ.

When you finally get beyond screaming, "These are my rights. I am going to get what's coming to me. I am hurt. I am lonely. I am depressed. Me, me, me!" you finally begin to see things through Christ's perspective. Life then begins to get good! The *lower* you bend in His presence, the *higher* He raises you into joy, peace and true life. It is a process. No one arrives overnight. Just hang in there. You will begin to see progress: a little victory here and then a greater victory there. On and on it will continue. Gradually Christ will become more and more in control, the self-will will dominate less and less. That is when you emerge from the cocoon of the caterpillar into being a butterfly. Life takes on new meaning. You can fly, swoop, spin and ascend towards the heights as never before.

*Remember*: Marriage reveals what is inside of you. Do not blame your character flaws on your husband and wife. You are what you are. Circumstances only divulge them. You can hide what you are from many people, but when you live with someone day in and day out, your true self emerges. This is why it is so important to put on Christ and not stay within the prison of self. Christ liberates, self condemns. Without Christ you can do nothing (John 15:5), but with Christ you can do all things (Philippians 4:13).

Jesus said, "Abide in me, and I in you...This is my commandment, That ye love one another, as I have loved you. Greater love hath no man than this, that a man lay down his life for his friends" (John 15:4,12-13).

A touching story was told about four-year-old Martha. Hugging a doll in each of her pudgy little arms, she looked wistfully up at her mother and said, "Mamma, I love them, but they never love me back." May these words never be spoken in your marriage, whether out loud or silently within the heart.

True love is described in I Corinthians 13:4-8. The word *charity* used in the King James Version has been replaced with the word *love* in the following admonition:

a. Love suffereth long.
b. Love is kind.

c.  Love envieth not.

d.  Love vaunteth not itself.

e.  Love is not puffed up.

f.  Love doth not behave itself unseemly.

g.  Love seeketh not her own.

h.  Love is not easily provoked.

i.  Love thinketh no evil.

j.  Love rejoiceth not in iniquity.

k.  Love rejoiceth in the truth.

l.  Love beareth all things.

m.  Love believeth all things.

n.  Love hopeth all things.

o.  Love endureth all things.

p.  Love never faileth.

Dwight Small wrote,

Eros must be transcended and transformed by agape, human love must be infused with divine love. This is possible when two persons bring their love to Christ. Through redemption the love of God comes into human life as mercy and grace, teaching the mystery and power of forgiving love in human relations. In returning love to Christ, husband and wife find their own love purified and strengthened. [12]

**Give reverence.**

The Bible goes a step further and instructs the wife to not only love her husband but to reverence him. Ephesians 5:33 states, "Let...the wife see that she reverence her husband."

Reverence is a feeling of deep respect, love and awe. To reverence him is to notice, regard, praise, honor, respect, prefer, venerate and esteem him. To reverence means to go beyond casual love and to admire him exceedingly! God knew that men had egos which needed to be stroked and built up from time to time. He made them that way. It is the duty of the wife to help fulfill that need and make her man feel *important* and *big*.

The wife should not be a shrill, screaming, ranting maniac, neither should she be as a cold, clammy fish. She should seek to be warm, gentle, kind and understanding. Love and attention are not luxuries; they are essential foods of marriage.

What does it mean to show respect and reverence to someone? Let the following story explain:

During the war between the states, General Lee one day sent word to Stonewall Jackson that the next time he rode in the direction of headquarters the Commander in Chief would be glad to see him on a matter of no great importance. General Jackson received the message and immediately prepared to leave the next morning. Rising very early, he rode the eight miles to Lee's headquarters against a storm of wind and snow, and arrived just as Lee was finishing breakfast. Much surprised, Lee inquired why Jackson had come through such a storm.

General Jackson replied: "But you said that you wished to see me. General Lee's slightest wish is a supreme command to me."

This is true reverence and respect: the slightest wish is a supreme command to the one who loves.

Some important things to remember:

- Love is not possessive.
- Make each other feel well-liked, not just tolerated.
- A compliment is a stimulant, a complaint is a depressant.
- Never tear each other down in front of other people.
- Grumbling is the death of love.
- *A word to the wives*: Learn the four A's:

  *Adapt* to your husband. Learn to like the things he likes (at least show interest).

  *Admire* him.

  *Accept* him. If you do not like the way he is, pray and ask God to change him.

  *Appreciate* him, for appreciation is the core of a beautiful marriage.

"And let the beauty of the Lord our God be upon us: and establish thou the work of our hands upon us; yea, the work of our hands establish thou it."

Psalm 90:17

# Establish

THE WORD *ESTABLISH* means "to make stable or firm; to fix immovably or firmly; settle. To set on a firm basis." If certain things are not established or settled, time marches on and life sifts through your fingers just like sand. The following areas should be discussed even before marriage, during the engagement period, and plans should begin on how to establish them:

**Establish goals.**

Because two people of two different mind-sets and personalities live together, it is necessary for them to come together and define immediate and long-range goals. Goals should be discussed that deal with spiritual growth, material needs, financial planning, each other's dreams or anything of interest to each other.

Dr. Maxwell Maltz, in his book *Psycho-Cybernetics,* says:

We are engineered as goal-seeking mechanisms. We are built that way. When we have no personal goal which we are interested in and which means something to us, we have to go around in circles, feel lost, and find life itself aimless and purposeless. We are built to conquer environment, solve problems, achieve goals, and we find no real satisfaction or happiness in life without obstacles to conquer and goals to achieve. People who say that life is not worthwhile are really saying that they themselves have no personal goals which are worthwhile. [1]

It is essential that husband and wife have periodic meetings for setting their goals. The Apostle Paul instructed Christians to "press toward the mark" (Philippians 3:13). You must know where you are going or you will never get there.

Harry Emerson Fosdick said, "No horse gets anywhere till he's harnessed, no steam or gas drives anything until it's confined, no Niagara ever turns anything into light or power until it's tunneled, no life ever grows great until focused, dedicated, and disciplined." [2]

## Establish an altar.

Two days before we were married, a card came in the mail addressed to both of us. The words, "Do not open until the day of the wedding," were penciled across the top. We thought there might be some money in it and waited excitedly to open it. On our wedding day, October 14, 1961, we tore the envelope open and found there was no money inside. We read the card and at the bottom were the words, "The family that prays together, stays together." The words *prays* and *stays* were underlined. The sender of the card was Rev. A.D. Urshan. He knew what was important.

Leo Tolstoy, the famous writer, wrote, "I believe it is impossible to live well without prayer, and that prayer is the necessary condition of a good, peaceful, and happy life. The Gospels indicate how one should pray, and what prayer should consist of." [3]

Abraham of the Old Testament knew how to pray and commune with God. God says of Abraham in Genesis 18:19, "For I know him, that he will command his children and his household after him, and they shall keep the way of the Lord, to do justice and judgment; that the Lord may bring upon Abraham that which He hath spoken of him."

Abraham was an altar builder. The scriptural references which prove this follow:

Genesis 12: 7: "And the Lord appeared unto Abram, and said, Unto thy seed will I give this land: and there *builded he an altar* unto the Lord, who appeared unto him."

Genesis 13:18: "Then Abram removed his tent, and came and dwelt in the plain of Mamre, which is in Hebron, and *built there an altar* unto the Lord."

Genesis 22:9: "And they came to the place which God had told him of; and Abraham *built an altar* there."

He not only built the altars but he visited them often. Genesis 13:4 says, "Unto the place of the altar, which he had made there at the first: and there Abram called on the name of the Lord."

It is important to establish a daily altar. If prayer is not made to the Lord, there will eventually be trouble, because self-will will triumph over self-discipline. Prayer does many good things for the home. Some of them are listed below:

1. Prayer causes a bond to be formed that is unbreakable; it builds, strengthens, and cements husband and wife together.
2. Prayer penetrates the subconscious and controls the conscious; it is power!
3. Prayer is the highest form of communication with God. For right communication to occur between husband and wife, there must first be communication with God.
4. Prayer gives new inspiration and lets you look at things differently. It helps takes your mind off the faults of your mate.
5. Family prayer may be likened to the roof of your home. If neglected, it will be as if removing one shingle at a time, exposing your family to pelting storms of sin and temptation. If you do not pray daily, your roof will gradually weaken, then

be destroyed, and your family will be bombarded by the world.

Do not be too big, prideful or sophisticated to pray. Many great people have learned the secret of prayer. President Abraham Lincoln, during the Civil War, said, "I have been driven many times to my knees by the overwhelming conviction that I had nowhere else to go. My own wisdom and that of all about me seemed insufficient for the day." [4]

"Prayer"

Lord, what a change within us one short hour
Spent in thy presence will prevail to make!
What heavy burdens from our bosoms take,
What parched grounds refresh as with a shower!
We kneel, and all around us seems to lower;
We rise, and all, the distant and the near,
Stands forth in sunny outline brave and clear;
We kneel, how weak! we rise, how full of power!
Why, therefore, should we do ourselves this wrong,
Or others, that we are not always strong,
That we are ever overborne with care,
That we should ever weak or heartless be,
Anxious or troubled, when with us is prayer,
And joy and strength and courage are with thee!

*Richard Trench* [5]

Where there is no prayer the soul is dead.

## Establish faithful church attendance.

Henry Ward Beecher said, "A world without a *Sabbath* would be like a man without a smile, like a summer without flowers, and like a homestead without a garden. It is the joyous day of the whole week." [6]

"Sunday is the golden clasp that binds together the volume of the week," was penned so beautifully by Henry Wadsworth Longfellow. [7]

## Establish time for reading the Bible.

J.W. Alexander illuminated the secret sought by all in the following statement: "The study of God's word, for the purpose of discovering God's will, is the secret discipline which has formed the greatest characters." [8]

Thomas Jefferson wrote, "I have always said, and always will say that the studious perusal of the sacred volume will make us better citizens, better fathers, and better husbands [and wives]." [9]

Marriages were designed by God to be happy and fulfilling, but they need God's guidance in order for this to be. The key to a happy marriage is to seek to know Jesus and be guided by His principles. There is judgment pronounced upon those who forsake the Lord. "They that forsake the Lord shall be consumed" (Isaiah 1:28). Forsake not the Lord, but build your life around Him and blessing and honor will be upon you.

If every husband and wife will establish the four points emphasized above and make them a priority in their home, they can anticipate their golden wedding anniversary. Knowing where they are going, praying together, worshipping at church together and reading the Bible together spells success. As the character of God is revealed unto them, they begin to take on His attributes and see things through His eyes. When God is included in the marriage and asked to be the Head, there will be success, for God always wins!

# EPILOGUE

"LIVING PROOF"

The question is asked, "Is there anything more beautiful in life than a boy and girl clasping clean hands and pure hearts in the path of marriage?"

And the answer is given, "Yes—there is a more beautiful thing; it is the spectacle of an old man and an old woman finishing their journey together on that path. Their hands are gnarled but still clasped; their faces are seamed but still radiant; their hearts are tired and bowed down but still strong. They have proved the happiness of marriage and have vindicated it from the jeers of cynics."

*Author unknown* [1]

# NOTES

Introduction

[1]   Paul Lee Tan, ThD., *Encyclopedia of 7,700 Illustrations: Signs of the Times* (Rockville, MD: Assurance Publishers, 1979), 3328.
[2]   Phyllis Hobe, edited by, *Dawnings* (Carmel, NY: Guideposts, 1981), 203.

Chapter 1

[1]   J. Allen Peterson, edited by, *The Marriage Affair* (Wheaton, IL: Tyndale House Publishers, 1971), 371.
[2]   Alice Reynolds Flower, *The Home* (Springfield, MO: Gospel Publishing House, 1955), 7.
[3]   Donald O. Bolander, M.A., Litt.D, compiled by, *The New Webster's Quotations* (Lexicon Publications, Inc., 1987), 114.
[4]   Arthur F. Lenehan, Ed., *Soundings, Vol. D/No. 7A*, (Fairfield, NJ: The Economics Press, 1988), 20.
[5]   Flower, 63.
[6]   Dean C. Dutton, Ph.D. D., arr. & comp., *Quests & Conquests* (Guthrie, OK: Live Service Publishing Co., 1923), 793.
[7]   Tan, 4751.
[8]   Walter B. Knight, *Knight's Treasury of Illustrations* (Grand Rapids, MI: Wm. B. Eerdmans Publishing Co., 1963), 167-168.
[9]   Joseph S. Johnson, comp., *A Field of Diamonds* (Nashville, TN: Broadman Press, 1974), 108.

[10]   Ibid.


Chapter 2

[1]   Dale Carnegie, *How to Win Friends & Influence People* (New York, NY: Pocket Books, 1936), 26.
[2]   Peterson, 343.
[3]   Tan, 3185.
[4]   Gary Smalley & John Trent, *The Blessing* (Nashville, TN: Thomas Nelson Publishers, 1986), 171-172.
[5]   Jack Canfield & Mark Victor Hansen, *Chicken Soup for the Soul* (Deerfield Beach, FL: Health Communications, Inc., 1993), 43-45.
[6]   Knight, 110.


Chapter 3

[1]   Carnegie, 143.
[2]   Peterson, 83, 85-86.
[3]   Bolander, 23.
[4]   Ibid., 177.
[5]   Peterson, 69.
[6]   Ibid.
[7]   Porter B. Williamson, *Patton's Principles* (New York, NY: Simon & Schuster, 1979), 14.


Chapter 4

[1]   Carnegie, 143.
[2]   Ibid., 146.
[3]   Bolander, 158.
[4]   Carnegie, 118.
[5]   Bolander, 177.
[6]   Ibid., 186.
[7]   *Bits & Pieces, Vol. N/No. 3*, (Fairfield, NJ: The Economics Press, Inc., 1941), 17-19.


Chapter 5

[1] Bolander, 176.
[2] Ibid.
[3] Knight, 8.
[4] Clinton T. Howell, ed., *Lines to Live By* (Nashville, TN: Thomas Nelson Publishers, 1972), 44.
[5] Knight, 356.
[6] Ibid., 355.
[7] Ibid., 353.
[8] Bolander, 189.
[9] Knight, 354.
[10] Dutton, 793.
[11] Knight, 178.

Chapter 6

[1] Don Aslett, *Make Your House Do the Housework* (Cincinnati, OH: Writer's Digest Books, 1986), 7.
[2] Ibid.
[3] Anne R. Free, *Social Usage*, (New York, NY: Appleton-Century-Crofts, 1960), 39.
[4] Peterson, 325.
[5] Bolander, 103.
[6] Peterson, 326.
[7] Ibid., 45.
[8] Knight, 240.
[9] Tan, 2354.
[10] Dutton, 190.
[11] Ibid., 472.
[12] Ibid., 310.
[13] Ibid., 287.
[14] Ibid., 85.
[15] Ibid., 63.
[16] Tan, 898.
[17] Dutton, 276.
[18] Ibid., 471.
[19] Ibid., 254.
[20] Ibid., 91.
[21] Ibid., 484.
[22] Edgar A. Guest, *Collected Verse of Edgar Guest* (Chicago, IL: Reilly & Co., 1934), 713-715.
[23] Dutton, 484.

Chapter 7

1   Bolander, 163.
2   Ibid., 180.
3   Ibid., 181.
4   Ibid.
5   Ibid., 201.
6   Knight, 114.
7   Peterson, 298.
8   Ibid., 114.
9   Knight, 116.

Chapter 8

1   Aslett, 34.
2   Bolander, 52.
3   Ibid., 76.
4   Ibid., 81.
5   Ibid., 217.
6   Ibid., 179.
7   Ibid., 59.
8   Tan, 420.
9   Bolander, 231.
10  Ibid., 209.
11  Peterson, 363.
12  Bolander, 10.
13  Ibid., 70.
14  Ibid.
15  Ibid.
16  Ibid.
17  Ibid.
18  Ibid.
19  Ibid.
20  Dutton, 483.
21  Bolander, 90.
22  Ibid., 67.
23  Ibid., 68.
24  Ibid., 75.
25  Ibid., 215.
26  Ibid., 163.
27  Joy Haney, *Women of the Spirit, Vol. III* (Stockton, CA: Radiant Life, 1996), 81.

28 Bolander, 219.
29 Johnson, 172.
30 Ibid.
31 Ibid., 793.

## Chapter 9

1 Bolander, 163.
2 Howell, 125.
3 Bolander, 174.
4 Dutton, 158.
5 Bolander, 203.
6 Tan, 3173.
7 Knight, 416.
8 Howell, 25.
9 Ibid., 23.
10 Ibid., 22.
11 Ibid., 23.
12 Ibid., 23.
13 Ibid., 25.
14 Ibid., 23.
15 Ibid., 25.
16 Ibid., 26.
17 Ibid., 157.
18 Dutton, 121.

## Chapter 10

1 Dutton, 254.
2 Ibid., 7.
3 Tan, 3907.
4 Dutton, 128.
5 Bolander, 65.
6 Ibid., 66.
7 Ibid., 66.
8 Dutton, 35.
9 Bolander, 31.
10 Ibid., 171.
11 Howell, 152.
12 Ibid., 12.

[13] Dutton, 1295.
[14] Ibid.
[15] Ibid.
[16] Ibid.
[17] Ibid.
[18] Ibid.
[19] Ibid.
[20] Ibid.
[21] Tan, 3788.
[22] Bolander, 22.
[23] Ibid., 203.
[24] Dutton, 130.
[25] Tan, 1800.
[26] Howell, 99.
[27] Dutton, 472.
[28] Ibid., 469.
[29] Ibid., 1340.

Chapter 11

[1] Dutton, 466.
[2] Bolander, 85.
[3] Ibid., 86.
[4] Ibid.
[5] Lenehan, 16.
[6] Haney, 57.
[7] Bolander, 41.
[8] Dutton, 57.
[9] Howell, 37.
[10] Dutton, 705.
[11] Ibid., 793.
[12] Ibid.

Chapter 12

[1] Bolander, 2.
[2] Ibid., 42.
[3] Ibid., 158.
[4] Willard F. Harley, Jr., *His Needs, Her Needs* (Grand Rapids, MI: Fleming H. Revell, 1994), 38.

5   Ibid. 40.
6   Morris Fishbein, M.D. & Ernest W. Burgess, Ph.D., *Successful Marriage* (Garden City, NY: Doubleday & Co., 1963), 88-89.
7   Ibid.
8   Ibid., 98-99.
9   Bolander, 8.
10  Ibid., 8.
11  Howell, 130.
12  Peterson, 87.

Chapter 13

1   Maxwell Maltz, M.D., F.I.C.S., *Psycho-Cybernetics* (New York, NY: Pocket Books, 1976), 114.
2   Peterson, 61.
3   Johnson, 153.
4   Ibid., 152.
5   Howell, 175.
6   Ibid., 170.
7   Ibid., 175.
8   Ibid., 172.
9   Dutton, 1361.

Epilogue

1   Johnson, 17.